GLUTEN-FREE
Entertaining

**MORE THAN 100 NATURALLY WHEAT-FREE RECIPES
PERFECT FOR ANY OCCASION**

OLIVIA DUPIN

FAIR WINDS
PRESS
BEVERLY, MASSACHUSETTS

First published in the USA in 2013 by
Fair Winds Press, a member of
Quayside Publishing Group
100 Cummings Center
Suite 406-L
Beverly, MA 01915-6101
www.fairwindspress.com

17 16 15 14 13   1 2 3 4 5

ISBN: 978-1-59233-579-4

Digital edition published in 2013
eISBN: 978-1-61058-880-5

Library of Congress Cataloging-in-Publication Data available

Cover and Book Design by Duckie Designs
Photography by Theresa Raffetto
Food Styling by Jessica Gorman and Olivia Dupin
Prop Styling by Deborah Williams

Printed and bound in China

To my family and friends.
I love having you around my table.

CONTENTS

3 SPECIAL OCCASIONS | 89

INTRODUCTION

Coming together with friends and family to enjoy a meal is one of the simplest pleasures in life. We pass on our traditions and create wonderful memories with the ones we love. Whether you are opening your home to celebrate holidays, special events, or "just because," entertaining for your honored guests should be as enjoyable for you as it is for them. The problem is, however, that oftentimes the stress and pressure of creating the perfect setting, cooking a delicious meal, and getting everything hot and on the table all at once can be extremely stressful. And if you are attempting to serve a completely *gluten-free* meal, you might find yourself even more intimidated.

A gluten-free diet eliminates wheat, barley, and rye, or foods that have come in contact with these ingredients. It sounds simple, but so many of us hear the words "gluten-free" and cringe. We've been conditioned to think gluten-free foods taste bad and require trips all over town hunting down specialty ingredients that cost a fortune. Not so. In this book, I'll show you how to create wonderful meals for entertaining without all those hard-to-find ingredients—and without the stress, too. With this book, featuring fourteen delicious menus, all with step-by-step timelines and instructions on what to prepare and when, you'll see how fun and easy entertaining can be. And oh yeah, every recipe in this book *is* gluten-free, but that's just a bonus!

Whether you live a gluten-free lifestyle or know others who do, this book will help ensure that the food you serve is delicious and enjoyable for *everyone*. As a chef with celiac disease, I can promise you that no one will know these delightful dishes are gluten-free unless you tell them—but I *can't* promise you won't want to brag!

1

Planning the Perfect Party

With a little preparation, planning the perfect party will be easier than you think.
I'll walk you through a few simple steps that will make your event memorable,
relaxing, and fun for everyone—even you!

Start with the Basics: The Date, the Guest List, and the Invites

Picking the date and guest list for your party can make or break an event. If your party is on a holiday, like Christmas, the date is set, and your guest list probably includes mostly close friends and family, so there's not much to worry about there. But if you're trying to throw a big blowout for your 30th birthday, then there may be more to consider. If the date falls over a long weekend when all your friends will be away, you may be disappointed with the turnout. So check your calendar, and ask around. Is someone in your social circle having something that same night? Keep these things in mind when picking the date.

When choosing the guest list for my parties, I first consider the space. A sit-down dinner at home can only accommodate as many guests as you can comfortably seat at your table. Decide how many people you'd like to have, then choose the guest list. I love to mix and match friends from different areas of my life to keep it interesting; inviting colleagues, my oldest friends from grade school, and my new neighbors from down the street, for instance, would make for interesting conversation and give all of my friends a chance to get to know each other.

Invitations can be as simple as a phone call inviting your guests over, or for a more formal event like a baby shower, you can send invitations. Send invitations several weeks in advance to give guests plenty of time to save the date for the party. Printed invitations are wonderful, but I find myself choosing online invitations more and more. They are less expensive (often free) and allow you to manage a guest list easily and quickly. You can view who has opened the invite and also send reminders to guests who haven't responded yet. My favorite online invites are from www.punchbowl.com and www.evite.com.

Plan the Menu

Planning a party is all in the details, and deciding on the menu can seem daunting. Fortunately, with this book, you're one step ahead of the game! I've put together some great menus that can be used as is, or even mixed and matched. There are a few things you'll want to consider before you begin, however, such as: How many people will be attending? What are the dietary restrictions of your guests? Would you prefer to serve a more formal plated meal, a casual family-style meal, or just finger foods that will allow guests to mingle? What time of year is the party? Which foods are in season and readily available at that time?

Once you've answered these questions you can begin to plan the menu. You'll want to serve a variety of foods that will appeal to everyone in your group, be easy to prepare, and be ready all at the same time. My secret is to always serve some items that can be made ahead and served cold or at room temperature and some items that can be partially prepped in advance and finished right before you eat. If you don't want to worry about serving cocktails, you can serve beer and wine, which don't require any prep (you can serve gluten-free beer and/or regular beer for guests who can tolerate gluten). If you're feeling ambitious, offer a mixed cocktail that complements the menu. A balance of these different kinds of items will make your job as a host that much easier and allow you to have time to enjoy your party, the guests, and the food!

Make Shopping Easy and Affordable

It's amazing the amount of money you can save if you know where to look! Personally, I'm the world's best online shopper. If I'm looking for a particular serving piece, specialty food item, or anything else, I can find it online! Websites like Amazon that offer customer reviews are key. Read them and use them to make sure you're really getting a quality product at a bargain instead of a cheap dud. Once I've found what I'm looking for (and before I check out), I do an online search for coupon codes (www.retailmenot.com is a great resource for this). You'd be amazed at what you can save this way, just by looking! Enter the coupon code at checkout; it's that easy.

Aside from online shopping, I also hit up my local savings club like Costco or Sam's Club for bulk party items. Deals here are exceptional. Doing a lot of baking? *This* is the place to stock up on butter, eggs, vanilla, powdered sugar, and more. Having a cocktail party? You can get your liquor here, too! And you'd be amazed at the prices on things like organic meats and poultry. I usually pay one-third of what I would at the local organic market. If you really want to save time and money there, though, heed this advice: Beware of temptation—there will be lots of bargains on items you don't *need* that will seem very tempting. Put your blinders on and walk on! You're not saving anything if you wind up spending what you save on impulse buys. Make a list and stick to it. Also, get there early or go late to avoid crazy lines.

Prep for the Party

It took me years to accept that I'm not Martha Stewart. When I used to entertain, I'd spend so much time and money trying to make every detail perfect, stressing out for a week just to throw a dinner for my friends, and running around cooking, serving, clearing, chasing around guests with coasters and napkins, and then cleaning and loading the dishwasher all while my guests were still around. I finally realized that everyone has less fun when I do this and I don't get to enjoy myself because I'm running around like mad, stressing that everyone's glass needs a refill and that the kitchen looks messy. My friends, who are there to spend time with me, only see a stressed-out version of myself, too busy to have a conversation and socialize. Once I let go of this notion that everything needed to be perfect, parties at my house were so much easier and enjoyable for everyone. I relax and have fun and everyone else does, too. The key to being a great hostess isn't perfection. It's about letting your parties reflect your own personality and style—not Martha's.

Set the Scene

Music, lighting, and décor all help set the scene for your event. Think about the mood you want to set and the feel you want your party to have. For most dinners and cocktail parties my formula is the same: simple flower arrangements in the main space where guests will be, plus one or two stems in a simple vase in each bathroom. I choose music that is fun and relaxed, but nothing too slow or sappy, which can give the party a sullen feel (I love services like Pandora and Spotify for this—they can help make selecting the music effortless). I use soft lighting and light *unscented* candles anywhere there will be food and drinks (scented candles can interfere with your sense of smell and taste, because the two are so closely linked). If you must use a scented candle anywhere, the bathroom is a great place! Additional details like pressed linen napkins can make your party feel extra special without a lot of effort. Does all of this sound like a lot to remember? If you do a lot of entertaining, these details eventually come as second nature, but if it just feels too fussy, remember: The most important thing is that your party reflects your own style, and that is what will make you and your guests have a great time. If you're a really casual entertainer, flowers in the bathroom might seem ridiculous to you and will feel pretentious to your guests. Just do what feels good and authentic for you!

How This Book Works

Each recipe in this book is part of a complete menu, but feel free to mix and match as you see fit. A salad from one chapter may be the perfect complement to another dish you've set your sights on making. The menus are only my suggested pairings—you are the boss in your kitchen! Use the index in the back of the book (page 170) to quickly search for recipes by type.

The timeline at the beginning of each menu gives wonderful suggestions on things you can prepare in advance. Do as much or as little in advance as you like. Each recipe also includes allergen labels, where applicable, outlining the top food allergens the recipe is free of (nuts, dairy, or soy). This will help you steer clear of any recipes that may have ingredients you'll need to avoid.

CREATING THE PERFECT FLOUR BLEND

In my first book, *The Complete Guide to Naturally Gluten-Free Foods*, none of the recipes used a flour blend. Very few used any flour at all, in fact, and consisted instead of recipes that were naturally gluten-free. Because entertaining is based on tradition and includes so many pies, cakes, and cookies, however, I knew I'd have to find a way to include some flour-based recipes here.

That said, I've never been a fan of cookbooks that tout their very own blend of flours because you're instructed to make a big batch, and then you can only really use it in the recipes in that *one* cookbook—which means it often winds up in a zipper bag lost in the back of your pantry never to be seen or used again. So I totally understand your hesitation to make *another* blend. But here's the difference: My simple blend consists of only three ingredients and can be made and used in two ways. You can either make a big batch of the blend, or you can measure out each of the three ingredients individually for each recipe, so nothing goes to waste. Each recipe states both measurement options. Be forewarned, though: This blend has a fantastic neutral flavor, gives baked goods a beautiful texture, and works brilliantly cup-for-cup (you may only need to reduce the liquid in your recipe slightly) in almost all of your gluten-containing recipes, so you might need more on hand than you think!

When I set out to make a blend, I was shocked to see the price tag on some of the "designer" gluten-free all-purpose flour blends on the market. One sold by a fancy retailer goes for about $20 for 3 pounds (1,350 g)! I knew I could do it for less, but I also wanted to develop a flour made only with ingredients that are easy to find, and that you could feel good about using. My blend has no xanthan gum, which can irritate sensitive stomachs, and is dairy-free, and because you make it yourself, you can control what goes into it. For instance, I highly recommend using non-GMO (genetically modified organism) cornstarch if you can. We're still learning about the dangers of genetically modified corn, but it has been shown to cause liver and kidney problems and cancer, and it has been banned in several countries outside of the United States. All organic cornstarch is non-GMO, and easy-to-find brands like Bob's Red Mill make a point of only using non-GMO corn for its cornstarch. I balance this blend with delicious and nutritious almond and oat flours, which can be purchased at most grocers, or easily made at home.

Almond flour, the second ingredient in my blend, can be made by grinding whole almonds, then sifting them through a fine-mesh strainer to remove any larger pieces. The larger pieces can be processed and sifted again until all of your almonds are a fine powder. Generally, I use raw, skin-on almonds in my recipes because the skins contain healthy flavonoids. Items baked with flour made from whole almonds will have some darker specks, giving it a "whole grain" look. If you prefer your baked goods to look like they were made with traditional all-purpose white flour, use blanched almonds, which are skinless and will give your food a more traditional look. You can find almond flour in some stores if you'd rather purchase it, but remember, almond *flour* is usually finer than almond *meal*, so do not confuse the two. Almond meal is usually sandy in texture while almond flour has a finer, more powdery consistency. If it's fine enough to pass through a fine-mesh sieve, then it's acceptable to use in these recipes.

Oat flour, my final flour ingredient, is simply finely ground oats. I like using oats because they are naturally gluten-free, but you have to make sure they were not processed in a facility that processes any gluten-containing ingredients because they can become contaminated. Gluten-free oats are usually found in the organic section of your local supermarket. You can find gluten-free oat flour in some stores as well, or you can make your own by grinding and sifting rolled or steel-cut oats in the same manner as for making almond flour.

For small jobs, my favorite tool to grind flours is a coffee grinder. Be sure to use a coffee grinder dedicated for this purpose only. A grinder used for coffee or spices will have lingering flavors that will affect your flours. A basic coffee grinder can be found at your local retailer for about $15, and this is the perfect choice if you don't do lots of baking. For bigger batches of almond or oat flour, a food processor works great; just pulse until all of the particles are fine, then sift and repeat if needed. Another wonderful tool is a high-powered blender, such as a Vitamix. Manufacturers of these blenders even offer special blender containers designed with blades meant specifically for grinding flours. But rest assured, you don't need expensive equipment to get the job done!

LIV'S FLOUR BLEND

•Soy-free •Dairy-free

This naturally gluten-free all-purpose blend is simply 2 parts cornstarch to 1 part almond flour and 1 part oat flour. If you'd rather not make a large batch, no worries—each recipe outlines the exact amounts of each ingredient.

4 cups (480 g) non-GMO cornstarch (organic if possible)

2 cups (240 g) almond flour (natural almond flour or blanched almond flour both work)

2 cups (240 g) oat flour (be sure to use gluten-free oats/oat flour)

Combine all the ingredients and store in the freezer to keep fresh. Because they don't contain any stabilizers, the flours may separate and settle as they sit. Give this a stir each time you pull it out to use.

Yield: 8 cups (960 g)

2

Celebrating the Holidays

The holidays are a time for family and friends to make memories and create special traditions. I've taken some quintessential holiday dishes and put a special twist on them. Not only are they gluten-free, but they are also better than ever! Be sure to refer to the timelines at the beginning of each menu to assist you in making the holidays stress-free and enjoyable with more of what matters—time with your loved ones!

New Year's Eve Cocktail Party

SERVES 6

New Year's Eve is one of my favorite fêtes. It's the time to reflect on the past year, and set goals for the new. Mostly it's a chance to celebrate hope and possibility for what's to come. I've selected some delicious appetizers and hors d'oeuvres for a cocktail-style party perfect for mingling guests, along with some festive cocktails to toast in the New Year right!

THE MENU

Countdown to the Party Timeline

2 DAYS BEFORE:

- ○ Make a list and do the grocery shopping.
- ○ Take out all platters, serving utensils, glasses, silverware, cocktail items, and plates that will be needed for the party as well as any decorations or centerpieces that you will need, such as candleholders, vases, linens, etc.
- ○ Make the Honey Dijon Roasted Chickpeas and store in an airtight container.
- ○ Make the cocktail sauce for the Shrimp Cocktail and refrigerate.
- ○ Make the Sun-Dried Tomato Crackers and store in an airtight container.
- ○ Write the messages that will go inside the Good Fortune Cookies.

1 DAY BEFORE:

- ○ Prepare the Parmesan and Almond Stuffed Dates and store in the refrigerator in an airtight container.
- ○ Make the Good Fortune Cookies and store in an airtight container.
- ○ Make the cornbread for the Cornbread Bites. Wrap tightly in plastic until ready to use.
- ○ Prepare the Warm Ricotta Dip, but do not bake. Wrap and refrigerate until ready to heat.

THE DAY OF:

- ○ Set the tables, bar area, and/or buffet and decorate as desired.
- ○ Poach the shrimp for the Shrimp Cocktail.
- ○ Make the Avocado Mousse for the Shrimp Cocktail.
- ○ Measure out and combine the ingredients for the Nutella Fondue, and set aside until ready to heat.
- ○ Prepare a platter with all ingredients that will be dipped into the fondue.
- ○ Cut strips of orange zest for the Manhattan cocktails.
- ○ Take out and arrange all the liquors and ingredients needed for the cocktails.
- ○ Sauté the andouille sausage and cut the cornbread for the Cornbread Bites.

1 HOUR BEFORE:

- ○ Arrange the Cornbread Bites with the cooked sausage on top on a sheet tray. Place in a 375°F (190°C, or gas mark 5) oven until warm, about 5-7 minutes.
- ○ Warm the ricotta dip in the oven.
- ○ Bring the stuffed dates to room temperature.
- ○ Place the shrimp on a platter with the cocktail sauce and Avocado Mousse.
- ○ Place the roasted chickpeas in a bowl.
- ○ Make the fondue using ingredients that have already been prepped.
- ○ Bring out the fortune cookies.

CORNBREAD BITES
WITH ANDOUILLE SAUSAGE

•Soy-free

Andouille is a smoked spicy sausage popular in Cajun cooking and is perfectly matched with my buttery cornbread. Use cooked hot Italian or chorizo sausage if you can't find andouille.

FOR CORNBREAD:

1 cup (140 g) masa harina

1 cup (140 g) medium-grind cornmeal

¼ cup (32 g) cornstarch

¼ cup (50 g) sugar

1 teaspoon baking powder

1 teaspoon baking soda

2 teaspoons salt

½ cup (112 g) unsalted butter, melted

1½ cups (355 ml) milk

2 large eggs

1 cup (130 g) fresh or frozen corn kernels (optional)

FOR TOPPING:

4 andouille sausages

¼ cup (60 g) sour cream

To make the cornbread: Preheat the oven to 425°F (220°C, or gas mark 7). Grease a 9 x 13-inch (23 x 33 cm) baking pan and set aside.

Combine the masa harina, cornmeal, cornstarch, sugar, baking powder, baking soda, and salt in a large bowl. Add the melted butter, milk, eggs, and corn kernels. Whisk until all of the ingredients are thoroughly combined. Pour the mixture into the prepared baking pan and bake for about 15 minutes, or until a toothpick inserted into the center of the bread comes out clean. Cool for 10 minutes, then invert onto a cutting board. Cut into 24 squares and place on a serving platter.

To make the topping: Cut each sausage into 6 pieces. Heat a sauté pan over high heat and brown the sausage pieces on each side by cooking for 2 to 3 minutes per side. Place 1 piece of sausage on top of each cornbread square, and top with ½ teaspoon dollop of sour cream. Serve warm or at room temperature.

Yield: 24 pieces

CHEF'S TIP

Masa harina is a corn flour used to make corn tortillas and can be found in the international section of most grocery stores.

PARMESAN AND ALMOND STUFFED DATES

•Soy-free

Dates are tender and sweet, truly nature's candy. Here they pair beautifully with a salty bite of Parmesan cheese and a crunchy almond, hidden away inside. Regular almonds will also work here, or try pistachios instead.

4 ounces (112 g) Parmesan cheese

24 pitted dates

24 blanched or Marcona almonds

Cut the Parmesan cheese into 24 small rectangles.

Use a paring knife to make a ½-inch (1.3 cm) slit in each date (through one side of the date, to the hollow where the pit was, not all the way through). Insert 1 almond into each date, then insert a piece of cheese, so that it's secured in the date, but sticking out of the top.

These can be made 1 day in advance if wrapped tightly and refrigerated. Bring to room temperature before serving.

Yield: 6 servings

HONEY DIJON ROASTED CHICKPEAS

•Soy-free •Dairy-free •Nut-free

Packed with protein and fiber, these crunchy, addictive chickpeas are a great alternative to roasted nuts. Honey and Dijon ensure your sweet and salty cravings are covered. Prepare to be addicted!

3½ cups (840 g) cooked chickpeas or 2 cans (15½ ounces, or 434 g each) chickpeas

1 tablespoon (15 ml) olive oil

¾ teaspoon salt

2 cloves garlic, lightly smashed

4 teaspoons honey

5 teaspoons Dijon mustard

Preheat the oven to 350°F (180°C, or gas mark 4). Drain and rinse the chickpeas (if using canned) and place on a rimmed baking sheet lined with parchment paper. Toss with the olive oil, salt, and garlic. Roast for about 1 hour, or until crunchy, stirring occasionally for even cooking.

Add the honey and Dijon mustard to the chickpeas, stir to coat the chickpeas evenly, and roast for 15 minutes longer, or until the coating is set but not too brown. Let cool and serve, or store in a resealable bag for up to 1 week.

Yield: 3 cups (720 g)

CHEF'S TIP

I love using any leftovers to top salads the next day!

SHRIMP COCKTAIL
WITH AVOCADO MOUSSE

•Soy-free •Dairy-free •Nut-free

Tender shrimp are paired with a duo of seriously spicy sriracha cocktail sauce and cool, creamy avocado mousse. Perfection!

2 pounds (908 g) large peeled and deveined shrimp, defrosted if frozen

FOR COCKTAIL SAUCE:

½ cup (120 g) ketchup

¼ cup (60 ml) sriracha

1 tablespoon (8 g) grated horseradish

1 tablespoon (15 ml) lemon juice

1 teaspoon honey

FOR AVOCADO MOUSSE:

1 clove garlic, minced

1 ripe avocado, peeled and pitted

1 tablespoon (15 ml) freshly squeezed lemon or lime juice

2 tablespoons (30 ml) water

Salt and pepper to taste

To make the shrimp: Fill a large stockpot with cold water and enough salt to make it taste like seawater. Cover and bring to a boil. Fill a large mixing bowl with ice and water. Add the shrimp to the boiling water and allow to cook for 3 minutes, or until just cooked through. Pour the shrimp into a colander to drain and add the shrimp to the cold ice water to stop the cooking and cool the shrimp. Drain again. Chill the shrimp until ready to use.

To make the cocktail sauce: Combine the ketchup, sriracha, horseradish, lemon juice, and honey in a medium-size bowl. Stir to combine. Chill until ready to use.

To make the avocado mousse: Combine the garlic, avocado, lemon juice, water, and a pinch each of salt and pepper in the bowl of a food processor. Process until smooth and creamy and light in texture. Chill until ready to use.

Serve the cocktail shrimp on a large platter with a small bowl of cocktail sauce and a small bowl of avocado mousse for dipping.

Yield: 6 servings

CHEF'S TIP

You can buy cooked shrimp and skip the poaching step to save time.

WARM RICOTTA DIP
WITH SUN-DRIED TOMATO CRACKERS

•*Soy-free*

This creamy and rich ricotta dip is begging for a crunchy cracker to scoop it up. The answer? My simple-to-make sun-dried tomato crackers. They are absolutely to die for, and grain-free, too!

FOR CRACKERS:

½ cup (55 g) sun-dried tomatoes in olive oil, drained

2 cups (240 g) almond flour

½ cup (50 g) finely grated Parmesan cheese

¼ teaspoon salt

FOR DIP:

1 pound (454 g) ricotta cheese

½ cup (50 g) finely grated Parmesan cheese, divided

2 teaspoons lemon zest

2 cloves garlic, finely minced

¼ cup (60 ml) milk

Preheat the oven to 350°F (180°C, or gas mark 4).

To make the crackers: Place the sun-dried tomatoes into a food processor and blend until very finely chopped. Place into a medium-size mixing bowl. Add the almond flour, Parmesan cheese, and salt and knead the mixture with your hands until it pulls together to form a ball.

Divide the dough in half. Place one half of the mixture on a sheet of parchment paper and top with another sheet of parchment paper. Use a rolling pin to roll the dough to about ⅛ inch (3 mm) thick. Remove the top piece of parchment paper. Gently slide the bottom piece of parchment with the dough onto a baking sheet. Use a sharp knife or a pizza cutter to cut the dough into 18 squares.

Repeat the rolling process with the other half of the dough.

Bake both sheets of crackers for about 14 minutes, or until lightly golden and crisp. Let cool before separating the crackers and serving.

To make the dip: Combine the ricotta cheese, Parmesan cheese, lemon zest, garlic, and milk in a food processor or mini food processor and pulse until creamy. Pour into a small baking dish and bake at 350°F (180°C, or gas mark 4) for 20 minutes, or until hot.

Yield: 36 crackers

CHEF'S TIP

Any hard cheese can be used to make the crackers. Experiment with manchego, Asiago, or Pecorino Romano instead.

GOOD FORTUNE COOKIES

•Soy-free

Better than takeout, these fortune cookies are extra special because you can fill them with custom fortunes containing well wishes for your friends and family for the New Year.

3 tablespoons (21 g) flaxseed meal

3 tablespoons (45 ml) boiling water

3 egg whites

¾ cup (150 g) sugar

¾ cup (90 g) Liv's Flour Blend (page 15) or *6 tablespoons (48 g) cornstarch plus 3 tablespoons (24 g) almond flour plus 3 tablespoons (24 g) oat flour*

1½ teaspoons vanilla extract

1 tablespoon (15 ml) heavy cream

4 tablespoons (56 g) unsalted butter, melted

⅛ teaspoon salt

Preheat the oven to 350°F (180°C, or gas mark 4). Generously grease 2 heavy cookie sheets. Cut out twenty-four 2½ x ½-inch (6.4 x 1.3 cm) pieces of paper and write fortunes on them.

In a small bowl, combine the flaxseed meal and boiling water. Let sit for 5 minutes so that the flax absorbs the water and forms a gel.

In a large bowl, beat the egg whites and sugar with a whisk until combined. Whisk in the flour blend, vanilla, heavy cream, melted butter, and salt. The consistency should resemble a crepe batter. Spoon the batter by tablespoonfuls onto the prepared baking sheet, 3 per sheet. Place one sheet in the oven to bake. In 3 minutes, place the other baking sheet in the oven.

Bake each tray for 6 to 8 minutes, or until the edges of the cookies begin to brown slightly and the centers look set. Use a small offset spatula to quickly lift one cookie at a time onto a clean, flat surface. Place a message in the center, and fold in half to cover the message. Fold the ends together the opposite way to form a fortune cookie shape. If they won't stay closed, place them under a drinking glass or coffee mug to hold the shape while they cool and set. When you've finished forming the first 3 cookies, the second sheet of cookies should be ready to come out of the oven and be shaped. Repeat the process until you have 24 fortune cookies.

Yield: 24 cookies

CHEF'S TIPS

- Dip the tips of the cookies in melted chocolate and dip in sprinkles to make these extra festive!
- If the cookies break in the center when you fold them, they probably haven't baked long enough. Make sure to bake until the edges are golden and the centers are set.

NUTELLA FONDUE

Fondue is one of my favorite things to make for a cocktail party. People love to pop by the fondue pot and dip, and it takes no time at all to prepare. Just remember to replenish the items meant for dipping from time to time!

¾ cup (180 ml) heavy cream

1 cup (175 g) chopped milk chocolate

1 cup (260 g) Nutella or other chocolate-hazelnut spread

2 tablespoons (30 ml) Frangelico

Fruit, marshmallows, and cookies, for dipping

Heat the cream in a small saucepan until just barely boiling. Remove from the heat, add the chopped milk chocolate, and stir until melted. Add the Nutella and Frangelico and stir to combine. Transfer to a fondue pot to keep warm and serve with the fruit, marshmallows, and cookies for dipping.

Yield: 6 servings

CHEF'S TIP
My Fluffy Marshmallows on page 74 are a great accompaniment to this chocolate-hazelnut heaven.

KIR ROYALE

•Soy-free •Dairy-free •Nut-free

Everyone needs something sparkly on New Year's Eve! This classic Champagne cocktail is splashed with crème de cassis, a sweet, jammy black currant liqueur.

....

1 teaspoon crème de cassis

⅔ cup (160 ml) sparkling wine or Champagne (enough to fill your champagne flute about three-fourths full)

Place the crème de cassis into a champagne flute and top with the sparkling wine.

Yield: 1 serving

CHEF'S TIP

Make this drink with white wine instead of Champagne and it's simply called a "Kir," also delicious!

MARASCHINO–LESS MANHATTAN

•Soy-free •Dairy-free •Nut-free

This cocktail originated in the 1800s. Shaken, not stirred, a classic Manhattan is also free of plastic-y artificial maraschino cherries. Some people prefer this drink over ice, so don't strain it if that is your preference.

....

¼ cup (60 ml) rye whiskey

1 tablespoon (15 ml) dry vermouth

1 or 2 dashes bitters (angostura bitters will do, but orange bitters are preferred)

1 strip orange zest (a "twist" of orange)

Place the whisky, dry vermouth, and bitters into a cocktail shaker with ice. Stir for 10 to 20 seconds to chill the drink. Strain into a martini glass and garnish with the twist of orange.

Yield: 1 serving

CHEF'S TIP

You can find orange bitters in most high-end liquor stores or kitchen supply stores.

Passover Seder

SERVES 6

Passover celebrates the Exodus of the Israelites from slavery in ancient Egypt. It is said that the Israelites fled Egypt in such a hurry that they didn't wait for their bread to rise, and made unleavened bread instead. Today, matzo, an unleavened cracker-like bread, is still eaten on Passover. This menu includes a fantastic g-free matzo and some other traditional foods with a great twist. Since this menu includes brisket, I've also included only sides and accompaniments that are dairy-free and pareve (meat- and dairy-free) in keeping with the kosher tradition.

....

THE MENU

Countdown to the Party Timeline

2 DAYS BEFORE:

- ○ Make a list and do the grocery shopping.
- ○ Take out all platters, serving utensils, glasses, silverware, cocktail items, and plates that will be needed for the party as well as any decorations or centerpieces that you will need, such as candleholders, vases, linens, etc.
- ○ Make the salad dressing and store in the refrigerator.

1 DAY BEFORE:

- ○ Make the Homemade Matzo. Store in an airtight container.
- ○ Make the Chocolate Chip Almond Torte. Wrap well with plastic and store at room temperature.
- ○ Set the table and decorate as desired.

THE DAY OF:

- ○ Make the Blackberry Wine Granita first thing in the morning and continue to scrape every 30 minutes or so until fully frozen.
- ○ Start preparing the Beef Brisket with Red Wine at least 4 to 5 hours before you will be serving dinner.
- ○ Prepare the Apple and Fig Charoset. Allow to rest at room temperature for at least 1 hour.
- ○ Prepare the Potato and Carrot Kugel. Wrap well with plastic and store in the refrigerator. Do not bake yet.
- ○ Chill dessert glasses in the freezer for the Blackberry Wine Granita.

1 HOUR BEFORE:

- ○ Take the plastic off of the kugel and bake in the oven as directed.
- ○ Take the lettuce out of the refrigerator and toss with the dressing right before serving.
- ○ Place foods onto serving platters and serve.

BITTER GREENS SALAD

•Soy-free •Dairy-free •Nut-free

Creamy tahini and herb dressing is just right with bitter greens. Any leftover dressing will keep nicely in the fridge for about 5 days.

FOR DRESSING:

2 garlic cloves, minced

¼ cup (60 g) tahini

⅔ cup (160 ml) fresh lemon juice

2 tablespoons (30 ml) water

½ cup (120 ml) extra-virgin olive oil

1 cup (40 g) packed fresh basil leaves

1 cup (60 g) packed fresh parsley

Salt and pepper to taste

8 cups (440 g) bitter lettuces such as romaine, chicory, escarole, radicchio, or watercress, washed and torn into bite-size pieces

To make the dressing: Combine the garlic, tahini, lemon juice, water, olive oil, basil, parsley, and a pinch each of salt and pepper in a food processor or blender. Blend until smooth and creamy.

Toss the desired amount of dressing with the greens and serve, or serve the dressing on the side and let guests dress their own salad.

Yield: 6 servings

CHEF'S TIP

A blender will give your dressing a smoother, creamier consistency while a food processor will leave this dressing with a little more texture. It's delicious both ways!

APPLE AND FIG CHAROSET

•Soy-free •Dairy-free

Charoset on the Passover table is meant to symbolize the mortar used by the Israelites to lay bricks when they were enslaved in Egypt. Often eaten plain or with matzo, this simple but essential element of the Passover table has the addition of dried figs for texture and interest.

3 medium-size apples, peeled, cored, and very finely diced

1 cup (150 g) dried figs, very finely diced

¾ cup (110 g) finely chopped roasted walnuts

¾ cup (180 ml) kosher red wine such as Manischewitz

½ teaspoon ground cinnamon

1 tablespoon (15 g) brown sugar

Combine all of the ingredients in a medium-size mixing bowl. Let sit for at least 1 hour to combine the flavors before serving.

Yield: 6 servings

POTATO AND CARROT KUGEL

•Soy-free •Dairy-free •Nut-free

**Creamy inside and crisp and brown on the outside, this kugel has
the addition of carrots for color and nutrition.**

5 tablespoons (75 ml) olive oil, divided

1 onion, diced

3 large russet potatoes (about 3 pounds [1,362 g]), peeled

1 pound (454 g) carrots, peeled and ends trimmed

1 onion, quartered

4 large eggs, lightly beaten

2 teaspoons salt

¼ teaspoon freshly ground black pepper

¼ cup (32 g) cornstarch

½ cup (120 ml) boiling water or chicken stock

Preheat the oven to 475°F (240°C, or gas mark 9).

Heat a small sauté pan over medium heat and add 1 tablespoon (15 ml) of the olive oil. Sauté the diced onion until caramelized, about 8 to 10 minutes. Set aside to cool slightly.

Meanwhile, grate the potatoes using the fine disk on your food processor. Grate the carrots, then grate the quartered onion in the same fashion. Place the grated vegetables into a colander set in your sink, and use the back of a spoon to squeeze out all the moisture that you can. Transfer to a large bowl.

Stir in the eggs, salt, pepper, caramelized onions, and cornstarch. Pour the boiling water over the mixture and stir to combine.

Pour the remaining ¼ cup (60 ml) oil into a 9 x 9-inch (23 x 23 cm) baking pan and heat in the oven for about 3 minutes, or until hot.

Carefully pour the potato mixture into the hot pan, place back into the oven, and bake for 20 minutes. Lower the heat to 400°F (200°C, or gas mark 6) and bake for an additional 40 minutes, or until the edges are crisp and the top is a dark, golden brown.

Yield: 6 servings

CHEF'S TIP

You want this to turn a deep golden brown, but if you feel it's getting too dark too quickly, cover the pan with foil and continue to cook as directed.

BEEF BRISKET
WITH RED WINE

•Soy-free •Dairy-free •Nut-free

This classic brisket gets just a touch of sweetness from the carrots and butternut squash. Be sure to slice your brisket across the grain of the meat to ensure tender, easy-to-eat bites that aren't stringy.

5 pounds (2,270 g) beef brisket

Salt and pepper to taste

1 tablespoon (15 ml) canola oil

4 cloves garlic, minced

1 onion, sliced into rings

1 pound (454 g) carrots, peeled and cubed

1 pound (454 g) butternut squash, peeled and cubed

¼ cup (32 g) cornstarch

3 cups (705 ml) dry red wine

1 cup (235 ml) beef broth

1 can (14½ ounces, or 406 g) diced tomatoes

1 bay leaf

Season the brisket generously on both sides with salt and pepper. Heat a large stockpot or Dutch oven over high heat. Add the canola oil, then sear the brisket for 4 to 5 minutes per side until golden brown. Transfer the brisket to a plate. Add the garlic, onion, carrot, and butternut squash to the pot. Dust with the cornstarch and stir to combine.

Add the red wine, beef broth, canned tomatoes, and bay leaf and stir. Return the brisket to the pot. Cover and simmer over medium heat until the liquid begins to softly boil. Reduce the heat to low and simmer, covered, for about 4 hours, or until tender when pierced with a fork.

Yield: 6 servings

CHEF'S TIP

Make this dish in a slow cooker by first searing the brisket in a sauté pan, then following the rest of the steps in your slow cooker. Cook on high for 4 hours.

ROASTED BEETS
WITH HORSERADISH

•Soy-free •Dairy-free •Nut-free

Roasted beets have a sweet, mellow flavor and are soft and tender. Their bright red color is a simply beautiful addition to your table.

1½ pounds (680 g) beets

1 teaspoon plus 2 tablespoons (30 ml) olive oil, divided

Salt and pepper to taste

2 tablespoons (14 g) prepared horseradish

1 clove garlic, finely minced

1 tablespoon (11 g) Dijon mustard

2 tablespoons (30 ml) red wine vinegar

Preheat the oven to 375˚F (190˚C, or gas mark 5).

Place the beets on a large piece of aluminum foil. Sprinkle with 1 teaspoon of the olive oil and salt, wrap tightly in the foil, and bake for about 1 hour, or until very tender when pierced with a fork.

Remove the beets from the oven and open the foil to release the steam. Let cool until the beets are cool enough to handle.

Meanwhile, make the vinaigrette for the beets by combining the horseradish, garlic, Dijon mustard, and red wine vinegar in a small bowl. Whisk thoroughly. Add the remaining 2 tablespoons (30 ml) olive oil and continue to whisk until fully incorporated.

Peel the beets with a paring knife. Cut them into ¾-inch (2 cm) cubes and place into a large bowl. Toss with the horseradish mixture, season with salt and pepper, then transfer to a serving dish and serve.

Yield: 6 servings

CHEF'S TIP

The beets should peel so easily that you may not need the paring knife at all; sometimes with a little rubbing the beets will slip right out of their skins! I use powder-free disposable gloves when handling beets to prevent staining my hands with beet juice.

CHOCOLATE CHIP ALMOND TORTE

•Soy-free •Dairy-free

This cake has a beautiful moist crumb and is quick to make. It's full of protein thanks to the almonds and the egg whites, so I don't feel guilty having the leftovers with coffee the next morning for breakfast!

5 egg whites, at room temperature

¼ teaspoon salt

¾ cup (150 g) sugar

3 cups (360 g) almond flour

¼ cup (60 ml) canola oil or trans-fat-free margarine, melted and cooled

2 teaspoons vanilla extract

1 cup (175 g) dark chocolate chips

Preheat the oven to 350°F (180°C, or gas mark 4). Lightly grease a 9-inch (23 cm) springform cake pan.

In a medium-size bowl, using an electric mixer, beat the egg whites, salt, and sugar until stiff peaks form. Use a rubber spatula to fold in the almond flour, oil, vanilla, and chocolate chips. Stir until just combined, taking care not to deflate the egg whites by overmixing.

Gently pour the mixture into the prepared pan. Bake for 35 minutes, or until golden and the sides begin to pull away from the pan.

Cool the cake on a rack, then run a knife around the edge of the pan to loosen the cake. Remove the rim of the springform pan and cool completely.

Yield: One 9-inch (23 cm) cake; 8 servings

CHEF'S TIP

To keep this cake pareve, be sure to use chocolate chips that are dairy-free!

HOMEMADE MATZO

•Soy-free •Dairy-free

**This recipe makes a wonderful neutral-flavored matzo with the perfect texture.
It's even easier to make gluten-free than it is to hunt them down
in your local specialty food store!**

4 cups (480 g) Liv's Flour Blend
(page 15) *or 2 cups (240 g)
cornstarch plus 1 cup (120 g)
almond flour plus 1 cup (120 g) oat
flour*

Cornstarch, for rolling

½ teaspoon salt

½ cup (120 ml) olive oil

½ to 1 cup (120 to 235 ml) water

Preheat the oven to 450°F (230°C, or gas mark 8).

Place the flour blend and salt in a food processor. Pulse to blend. Add the olive oil and ½ cup (120 ml) of the water. Pulse until the dough comes together. If it's crumbly, add a bit more water until a stiff dough forms. Continue to run the machine until the dough forms a firm ball that sticks to the blade.

Divide the dough into 6 even pieces. Dust a piece of parchment paper with cornstarch. Place a piece of dough on top and dust with more cornstarch. Top with a second piece of parchment paper and use a rolling pin to roll each piece of dough into an 8-inch (20 cm) circle that is very thin. Remove the top piece of parchment and slide the bottom piece onto a baking sheet.

Bake for 7 to 8 minutes, or until crisp and golden around the edges. Repeat the rolling and baking process with all of the dough and let cool completely before serving.

Yield: 6 large matzos

CHEF'S TIP

Use a dry pastry brush to dust any excess cornstarch off of the matzo before baking.

BLACKBERRY WINE GRANITA

•Soy-free •Dairy-free •Nut-free

A granita is like a grown-up snowcone. This frozen dessert will make a delicious and unexpected addition to your table. No one will believe the granita only has three ingredients!

1 cup (235 ml) water

1 cup (150 g) sugar

1 bottle (750 ml) blackberry wine such as Manischewitz, chilled

1 pint (290 g) fresh blackberries (optional)

Place a 9 x 13-inch (23 x 33 cm) metal baking pan in the freezer for 1 hour to chill.

Bring the water to a boil in a saucepan, turn off the heat, add the sugar, and stir to dissolve to make a simple syrup. Allow to cool completely. Combine the simple syrup and wine in the baking pan and return it to the freezer.

Scrape the frozen parts of the wine mixture with a fork every 30 minutes to create small ice crystals. The mixture should be soft, like snow, not frozen solid like an ice pop. Serve in dessert dishes and garnish with fresh blackberries.

Yield: 6 servings

CHEF'S TIP

Chill your dessert dishes in the freezer before serving to keep the granita from melting too quickly as you portion it out and serve.

Easter Brunch

SERVES 6

At our house, the Easter tradition was an egg hunt for mini foil-wrapped chocolate eggs. As a kid it seemed like there were millions scattered all over the house, and whoever found the most won a little prize, but of course the real prize was getting to enjoy all of that chocolate! This easy brunch menu features a bounty of spring produce, and has lots of make-ahead items so you can relax and enjoy *your* Easter morning traditions.

....

THE MENU

Countdown to the Party Timeline

2 DAYS BEFORE:

○ Make a list and do the grocery shopping.

○ Take out all platters, serving utensils, glasses, silverware, cocktail items, and plates that will be needed for the party as well as any decorations or centerpieces that you will need, such as candleholders, vases, linens, etc.

○ Plan the table setting, centerpieces, and décor.

○ Prepare the simple syrup for the Spiked Iced Coffee.

1 DAY BEFORE:

○ Set the table.

○ Make the raspberry purée for the Greek Yogurt Banana Splits.

○ Blanch the asparagus and make the citrus vinaigrette for the Asparagus with Shallots and Citrus Vinaigrette, but do not combine them.

○ Make and refrigerate the crust for the Deep-Dish Artichoke, Brie, and Ham Quiche.

THE DAY OF:

○ Make the waffle batter, but don't add the strawberries yet.

○ Dice the strawberries for the waffles.

○ Finish making the Deep-Dish Artichoke, Brie, and Ham Quiche.

○ Brew strong coffee and let cool, for the Spiked Iced Coffee.

1 HOUR BEFORE:

○ Make the Ginger and Apricot Smoothies.

○ Assemble the Spiked Iced Coffee.

○ Prepare the Greek Yogurt Banana Splits.

○ Toss together the asparagus and citrus vinaigrette.

○ Make the waffles right as guests begin to arrive.

○ Warm the quiche in the oven, if desired.

DEEP-DISH ARTICHOKE, BRIE, AND HAM QUICHE

•*Soy-free*

Tender artichokes, salty ham, and pungent Brie are enveloped by a creamy, savory custard in this beautiful quiche. A perfect tender crust makes it even more memorable.

FOR CRUST:

2 cups (240 g) Liv's Flour Blend (page 15) *or 1 cup (128 g) cornstarch plus ½ cup (60 g) almond flour plus ½ cup (60 g) oat flour*

½ teaspoon salt

⅛ teaspoon baking powder

9 tablespoons (126 g) cold unsalted butter, diced

2 tablespoons (30 ml) vodka

4 to 5 tablespoons (60 to 75 ml) ice water

FOR FILLING:

7 large eggs

1 cup (235 ml) milk

1 cup (235 ml) cream

¼ teaspoon grated nutmeg

¼ cup (25 g) grated Parmesan cheese

1 clove garlic, finely minced

½ teaspoon salt

¼ teaspoon freshly grated black pepper

⅔ cup (100 g) diced ham

1½ cups (450 g) cooked, diced artichoke hearts or 1 can (14 ounces, or 392 g) artichoke hearts, rinsed, drained, and diced

4 ounces (112 g) Brie, diced

Preheat the oven to 375°F (190°C, or gas mark 5).

To make the crust: Combine the flour blend, salt, and baking powder in the bowl of a food processor and pulse to combine. Add the cold butter, and pulse until the butter is the size of small peas. Add the vodka and 1 tablespoon (15 ml) of the water and pulse 1 or 2 more times. Continue adding 1 tablespoon (15 ml) water and pulsing until the dough just begins to hold together but is still slightly crumbly.

Turn out onto a sheet of parchment paper dusted with cornstarch and knead 2 or 3 times to bring the dough together into a ball. Roll the dough into a 12-inch (30 cm) circle, about ⅛ inch (3 mm) thick. Use a pastry brush to dust off any excess cornstarch from the crust, then use the parchment to transfer the dough into a deep-dish pie plate. Trim the edges of the crust to overhang by only ¼ inch (6 mm), then fold the edge under and press with your fingers to make a decorative edge. Pierce the bottom of the crust all over with a fork to prevent bubbles. Parbake the crust for 12 minutes, then set aside.

To make the filling: In a large bowl, whisk together the eggs, milk, cream, nutmeg, Parmesan cheese, garlic, salt, and pepper. Add the ham, artichokes, and Brie and stir to combine. Pour into the parbaked pie crust and bake for 35 to 40 minutes, or until the center of the quiche is set. Let cool and serve at room temperature.

Yield: 8 servings

CHEF'S TIP

The crust could be made ahead of time, patted into a disk, and stored in the refrigerator for 3 days or in the freezer for 1 month. Defrost overnight in the refrigerator before rolling it out.

ASPARAGUS AND SHALLOTS
WITH CITRUS VINAIGRETTE

•Soy-free •Dairy-free •Nut-free

Although it is often served as a hot side dish, asparagus is also fantastic cold. This light salad really highlights the fresh flavor of crisp, spring asparagus.

2 bunches asparagus

2 tablespoons (30 ml) lemon juice

3 tablespoons (45 ml) freshly squeezed orange juice

1 tablespoon (11 g) Dijon mustard

1 tablespoon (20 g) honey

3 tablespoons (45 ml) olive oil

Salt and pepper to taste

2 shallots

Bring a large saucepan full of salted water to a boil. Place a large bowl of ice water nearby. Cut the tough bottom 2 to 3 inches (5 to 7.5 cm) off of the asparagus stalks and blanch in the boiling water for 2 minutes. Shock in the cold water until cooled, then drain and pat dry with paper towels. Place into a serving dish and set aside.

In a small bowl, whisk together the lemon and orange juices, Dijon mustard, and honey. Drizzle in the olive oil and whisk until thoroughly blended. Season to taste with salt and pepper. Slice the shallots into thin rings, toss them with the dressing, and spoon over the asparagus spears.

Yield: 6 servings

CHEF'S TIP

Make this a quick light meal by serving with a piece of grilled chicken, fish, or tofu for a vegetarian version.

GREEK YOGURT BANANA SPLITS

•Soy-free

Greek yogurt is regular yogurt with water strained out, which makes it thicker. Using Greek yogurt in this banana split is indulgently creamy without all the extra sugar and fat that you get with your typical ice cream sundae, so it's perfect for brunch! No one will be able to resist.

1 pint (250 g) fresh raspberries

6 bananas

2 cups (460 g) plain Greek yogurt

4 tablespoons (85 g) honey, divided

¾ cup (83 g) sliced almonds, divided

Make the raspberry purée by placing the raspberries in a food processor and processing until liquefied.

Split each banana in half and place 2 halves onto 6 plates. Use an ice cream scoop to put 2 scoops of Greek yogurt onto each plate between the banana halves. Top one scoop with the raspberry purée. Top the other scoop with 2 teaspoons honey and 2 tablespoons (14 g) almonds. Repeat for each banana split, then serve.

Yield: 6 servings

CHEF'S TIP

• If fresh raspberries are not available, you can use frozen raspberries that have been thawed.

• For a smoother raspberry sauce, strain out the seeds with a fine mesh strainer.

DOUBLE STRAWBERRY WAFFLES

•Soy-free

These crisp, fluffy waffles get a double dose of strawberries with some mixed into the batter and fresh strawberries served on top. The waffle batter could be prepared one day in advance, but only mix in the strawberries right before they go into the waffle iron.

2⅔ cups (320 g) Liv's Flour Blend (page 15) *or 1⅓ cups (170 g) cornstarch plus ⅔ cup (80 g) almond flour plus ⅔ cup (80 g) oat flour*

1 teaspoon baking soda

1 teaspoon salt

2 eggs

½ cup (120 ml) cream

1 cup (235 ml) well-shaken low-fat buttermilk

4 tablespoons (112 g) unsalted butter, melted

1 teaspoon vanilla extract

3 cups (510 g) diced strawberries, divided

Maple syrup, for serving

Combine the flour blend, baking soda, and salt in a large bowl. Whisk in the eggs, cream, buttermilk, butter, and vanilla. Gently stir in 1 cup (170 g) of the diced strawberries.

Cook according to your waffle maker's instructions. Repeat with the remaining batter to make 6 waffles. Top them with the remaining 2 cups (340 g) strawberries and serve with the maple syrup.

Yield: 6 Belgian waffles

CHEF'S TIP

Substitute any berry that you prefer, or even chocolate chips!

GINGER AND APRICOT SMOOTHIES

•Soy-free

Smoothies are always a huge hit at brunch. I like to serve these in small juice glasses
right as guests begin to arrive to start off the meal with a sweet sip
of these healthy, gingery smoothies.

1 teaspoon freshly grated ginger

8 dried apricots

4 dates

½ cup (115 g) plain Greek yogurt

2 cups (470 ml) almond milk

10 ice cubes

Place all of the ingredients into a blender and blend on high until smooth
and creamy. Pour into six 6-ounce (180 ml) juice glasses and serve.

Yield: 6 servings

CHEF'S TIP

To make this dairy-free, replace the yogurt with coconut milk.

SPIKED ICED COFFEE

•Soy-free

Regular coffee gets a twist in this iced coffee and amaretto-spiked brunch cocktail. I serve
this in a pitcher, and let guests sweeten their drink to taste with a little pitcher of simple
syrup. If you have big coffee drinkers in your midst, consider doubling this to make two
pitchers of iced coffee.

FOR SIMPLE SYRUP:

½ cup (100 g) sugar

½ cup (120 ml) water

FOR ICED COFFEE:

3 cups (705 ml) cold strongly
brewed coffee

¾ cup (180 ml) amaretto

½ cup (120 ml) half-and-half

Ice

To make the syrup: In a small saucepan, combine the sugar and water and
stir well. Bring to a boil, and stir to make sure all the sugar has dissolved,
then remove from the heat. Let cool, then pour into a small pitcher.

To make the iced coffee: Pour the coffee, amaretto, and half-and-half
into a pitcher, stir, and top with ice. Serve with the simple syrup on the side
so guests can sweeten their own drink.

Yield: 6 servings

CHEF'S TIP

For the tea drinkers, make strong Earl Grey tea. Use the same method and
ingredients as for the coffee, but substitute Grand Marnier for the amaretto.

Giving Thanks Celebration

SERVES 6

Gluten-free never tasted so good! I've pared down the huge roasted turkey to just the breast, rolled it, and stuffed it with the perfect g-free stuffing, then complemented it with a whole pile of your favorite Thanksgiving staples, each with a twist you'll love. My party timeline makes it effortless, giving you even more to be thankful for!

....

THE MENU

Countdown to the Party Timeline

2 DAYS BEFORE:

○ Make a list and do the grocery shopping.

○ Take out all platters, serving utensils, glasses, silverware, cocktail items, and plates that will be needed for the party as well as any decorations or centerpieces that you will need, such as candleholders, vases, linens, etc.

○ Make the Chipotle-Tangerine Cranberry Sauce.

○ Make the cakes and the custard filling for the Mile-High Chocolate Cake but do not assemble. Store the cakes tightly wrapped in plastic at room temperature, and refrigerate the custard.

○ Bake 1 batch of the Super Quick Rosemary and Garlic Dinner Rolls on page 84 in a 9 x 13-inch (23 x 33 cm) pan for the Sausage and Apple Stuffing, wrap tightly in plastic, and store at room temperature.

1 DAY BEFORE:

○ Prepare the brine for the turkey and place the turkey breast in the brine overnight.

○ Make the Sausage and Apple Stuffing, but do not bake.

○ Make the Wholesome Pecan Pie and store at room temperature.

○ Prepare the Green Bean and Bacon Casserole, but do not bake or prepare the shallot topping.

○ Set the table, and decorate as desired.

THE DAY OF:

○ Assemble the cake with the custard, and store in the refrigerator.

○ Make the Honey Butter Creamed Corn.

○ Prepare the Candied Yams, but do not top with praline topping. Make the topping and store in the refrigerator.

○ Prepare and stuff the turkey, then put it in the oven to roast for 3½ hours before guests arrive.

1 HOUR BEFORE:

○ Prepare and fry the shallots for the green bean casserole.

○ Put the green bean casserole in the oven to bake.

○ Top the candied yams with the praline and place in the oven to finish baking.

○ Heat the creamed corn on the stove top before serving.

○ Make the Sage Gravy.

○ One hour before dessert is served, take the cake out of the refrigerator and dust with powdered sugar.

ROASTED TURKEY BREAST

•Soy-free •Dairy-free

A stuffed turkey breast is a great alternative to roasting a whole turkey for those who don't need such a large bird. Ask your butcher to debone your turkey breast for you, but leave the skin on.

FOR BRINE:

4 cups (940 ml) boiling water

¼ cup (60 g) brown sugar

⅓ cup (96 g) kosher salt

2 (2-inch, or 5 cm) pieces orange peel

1 tablespoon (5 g) black peppercorns

2 bay leaves, crushed

4 cups (940 g) ice cubes

4-pound (1.8 kg) boneless turkey breast

FOR ROASTING PAN:

1 onion, roughly chopped

1 rib celery, roughly chopped

4 cloves garlic

½ cup (120 ml) chicken stock, white wine, or water

FOR STUFFING:

1 batch Sausage and Apple Stuffing (page 54)

To make the brine: In a saucepan combine the water, brown sugar, salt, orange peel, black peppercorns, and bay leaves, and bring to a boil until the sugar and salt have dissolved. Take off the heat and add the ice cubes to cool the brine. When the brine is cold, combine the brining liquid and the turkey breast in a brining bag or large bowl. Brine the turkey overnight in the refrigerator.

Drain, rinse, and pat the turkey breast dry. Set aside.

To prepare the roasting pan: In a roasting pan combine the onion, celery, garlic, stock, and wine or water.

To stuff the turkey: Preheat the oven to 350˚F (180˚C, or gas mark 4). Place the turkey skin-side down on a clean work surface. Spread about 4 cups (520 g) of the stuffing evenly down the center of the turkey breast and roll the turkey around the filling. Use 4 lengths of kitchen twine to tie the turkey and secure the roll, pushing any stuffing that may fall out back into the roll. Place the turkey breast seam-side down in the prepared roasting pan.

Put the remaining stuffing in a separate greased baking dish and set aside. Roast the turkey for about 3 hours, or until it reaches an internal temperature of 160˚F (71˚C). The remaining stuffing should bake for 30 minutes. Place it in the oven at the end of your roasting time.

Transfer the turkey to a cutting board, and tent the turkey with aluminum foil to rest and stay warm while you make the gravy on page 54. Once you've prepared the gravy, remove the twine, slice the turkey breast, and serve on a platter with the gravy and stuffing on the side.

Yield: 6 servings

CHEF'S TIPS

If you aren't using a brining bag, be sure to use a nonreactive vessel (glass, plastic, stainless steel, ceramic, or enamel) for brining the turkey. Aluminum, cast iron, and copper are reactive metals that can leave a strong metallic flavor behind.

SAUSAGE AND APPLE STUFFING

•Soy-free •Dairy-free

This classic stuffing is good enough to rival any gluten-containing version!

....

1 batch Super Quick Rosemary and Garlic Dinner Rolls (page 84), baked in a 9 x 13-inch (23 x 33 cm) pan

½ pound (227 g) uncooked breakfast sausage or sweet Italian sausage, casings removed

2 cups (320 g) diced white onion

1 green apple, peeled, cored, and diced

1 cup (120 g) diced celery

1 tablespoon (2 g) ground sage

1 tablespoon (2.7 g) fresh thyme leaves

1 teaspoon salt

1 teaspoon freshly ground black pepper

2 eggs

3 cups (705 ml) chicken stock

Preheat the oven to 300°F (150°C, or gas mark 2). Cut the rosemary garlic bread into 1-inch (2.5 cm) cubes. Spread the cubes out on a sheet pan and toast in the oven for 15 minutes. Set aside to cool.

In a large sauté pan over medium heat, sauté the sausage until golden brown, about 5 minutes. Drain any excess fat from the pan, then add the onion, apple, celery, ground sage, thyme, salt, and pepper. Sauté until the vegetables have softened and the onions are translucent, about 5 minutes. Transfer to a large bowl and toss with the bread cubes. Whisk together the eggs and stock and toss with the bread cube mixture. Cook the stuffing with the Roasted Turkey Breast according to the directions on page 53.

Yield: 6 servings

CHEF'S TIP

The eggs in this stuffing are optional but will help bind the stuffing together and keep it from getting crumbly.

SAGE GRAVY

•Soy-free •Nut-free

This easy gravy is made directly in your roasting pan. Puréeing the gravy with the veggies from the pan maximizes the flavor of your gravy and ensures no lumps!

....

Roasting pan with drippings and vegetables from the Roasted Turkey Breast (page 53)

3 tablespoons (24 g) cornstarch

2 cups (470 ml) chicken stock

Salt and pepper (optional)

1 tablespoon (15 ml) heavy cream (optional)

2 tablespoons (5 g) chopped fresh sage

Heat the roasting pan with drippings over medium-high heat. Sprinkle in the cornstarch and cook, stirring, for 1 minute. Slowly whisk in the chicken stock. Bring the mixture to a boil while continuously whisking, about 2 to 3 minutes. Once the gravy has thickened, transfer the mixture to a blender and purée until smooth. Season with salt and pepper if needed, and stir in the heavy cream. Add the sage and serve hot.

Yield: 6 servings

CANDIED YAMS
WITH PECAN PRALINE

•Soy-free

The canned version of candied yams is loaded with corn syrup. Mine uses brown sugar and has tons of added flavor from the orange juice and zest.

FOR YAMS:

3½ pounds (1.6 kg) sweet potatoes

1 tablespoon (6 g) orange zest

½ cup (120 ml) freshly squeezed orange juice

1 cup (225 g) packed brown sugar

2 tablespoons (28 g) unsalted butter, diced

¼ teaspoon salt

FOR TOPPING:

1 tablespoon (15 ml) lightly beaten egg white

1 tablespoon (15 ml) heavy cream

¼ cup (60 g) brown sugar

1 tablespoon (8 g) cornstarch

½ teaspoon salt

1½ cups (150 g) pecans, chopped

To make the yams: Preheat the oven to 350˚F (180˚C, or gas mark 4). Peel the sweet potatoes and cut them into a large dice. Place in a 9 x 9-inch (23 x 23 cm) baking dish. Add the orange zest and juice, brown sugar, butter, and salt, and stir to combine. Bake for 1½ hours, stirring occasionally.

To make the topping: Combine the egg white, heavy cream, brown sugar, cornstarch, salt, and pecans in a small bowl. Pour over the yams and bake an additional 10 to 15 minutes, until the nuts are toasted and golden.

Yield: 6 servings

CHEF'S TIP

Skip the topping and use mini marshmallows if that's tradition in your home!

GREEN BEAN
AND BACON CASSEROLE

•Soy-free •Nut-free

Canned cream of mushroom soup is full of MSG and gluten! This classic holiday dish is easy to make from scratch and is everything a green bean casserole should be: creamy with tender green beans, and a crunchy shallot topping. Bacon only makes it that much better!

FOR TOPPING:

¼ cup (60 ml) canola oil

2 tablespoons (16 g) cornstarch

¼ teaspoon salt

⅛ teaspoon freshly ground pepper

2 shallots, thinly sliced into rings

FOR GREEN BEANS:

1 pound (454 g) green beans

6 strips bacon

1 package (10 ounces, or 280 g) button mushrooms, quartered

½ cup (80 g) diced white onion

3 cloves garlic, minced

3 tablespoons (24 g) cornstarch

1 cup (235 ml) chicken stock

½ cup (120 ml) heavy cream

Salt and pepper to taste

Preheat the oven to 350°F (180°C, or gas mark 4). Grease a 9-inch (23 cm) baking/serving dish and set aside.

To make the topping: Heat the canola oil in a small saucepan to 350°F (180°C) on a deep-fry thermometer. Mix together the cornstarch, salt, and pepper. Dust the shallots in the cornstarch and fry until crispy and golden, about 3 minutes. Use a slotted spoon to transfer the shallots to a plate lined with paper towels and set aside until ready to use.

To make the green beans: Bring a large pot of salted water to a boil over high heat. Add the green beans and cook for about 3 minutes (they should still be slightly crisp and bright green). Shock the beans in cold water, drain, and set aside.

In a medium sauté pan over medium high heat, sauté the bacon for about 4 minutes, until it just begins to turn crisp and golden. Drain all of the excess bacon fat except about 1 tablespoon (15 ml). Add the mushrooms to the pan and cook until they have released their juices and have browned, about 5 minutes. Add the onion and garlic, and cook until softened, about 2 minutes. Stir in the cornstarch and mix to coat everything evenly, then slowly whisk in the chicken stock and cream. Season with salt and pepper and cook until thickened. Mix in the blanched green beans. Pour into the prepared baking dish. Top with the shallots. Bake for 20 to 25 minutes, or until hot and bubbly.

Yield: 6 servings

CHEF'S TIP

Don't like green beans? Get creative and use broccoli, artichokes, brussels sprouts, or cauliflower.

HONEY BUTTER CREAMED CORN

•Soy-free •Nut-free

Fresh corn has lots of natural sweetness and a nice firm texture, making it perfect for delicious creamed corn, but frozen corn can be substituted here in a pinch.

3 ears corn (about 3 cups [450 g] kernels)

1 tablespoon (15 ml) olive oil

½ cup (80 g) diced white onion

½ cup (120 ml) chicken stock or water

½ cup (120 ml) heavy cream

⅛ teaspoon turmeric (optional)

¼ cup (35 g) medium-grind cornmeal

¼ cup (80 g) honey

3 tablespoons (42 g) cold unsalted butter

Salt and pepper to taste

Hold an ear of corn over a large bowl. Use a sharp knife to cut the kernels off of the corn cobs, then run the back of the knife along the cob to release any remaining liquid and "milk" the corn cobs. Discard the cobs, and set aside the corn and liquid.

Heat a large saucepan over medium heat. Add the olive oil and onion and cook for 3 to 5 minutes, or until softened and translucent. Add all of the corn kernels and any accumulated liquid to saucepan. Add chicken stock, cream, and turmeric. Bring to a boil. Slowly stir in the cornmeal while whisking, and then add the honey. Cook for 20 minutes, stirring occasionally. Whisk in the cold butter until melted. Season to taste with salt and pepper. Serve.

Yield: 6 servings

CHEF'S TIP
Turmeric in this recipe is optional but gives the corn a nice golden color.

CHIPOTLE–TANGERINE CRANBERRY SAUCE

•Soy-free •Dairy-free •Nut-free

This cranberry sauce hits all of your taste buds. It's great on sandwiches too.

12 ounces (280 g) fresh or frozen cranberries

2 tangerines, zested, then peeled and segmented without the pith

1 small chipotle pepper in adobo sauce, finely minced

¼ cup (60 ml) water

½ cup (112 g) brown sugar

1 cinnamon stick or ¼ teaspoon ground cinnamon

2 star anise pods

Combine the cranberries, tangerine zest and segments, chipotle pepper, water, brown sugar, cinnamon, and star anise in a large saucepan over medium heat. Bring to a boil, then reduce to a simmer and cook for 20 to 25 minutes, or until the cranberries have burst and the liquid is reduced and thickened. Remove the cinnamon stick and star anise pods. Cool to room temperature and serve.

Yield: 6 servings

WHOLESOME PECAN PIE

•Soy-free

Corn syrup has a flat sweetness, but maple syrup, brown sugar, and molasses give this pecan pie its rich caramel flavor. Plus, a requisite for any pie worth making? It's deep dish!

1 recipe pie crust (page 45)

1 cup (235 ml) maple syrup

⅔ cup (150 g) light brown sugar

1 tablespoon (20 g) molasses

3 tablespoons (42 g) unsalted butter

½ teaspoon salt

⅔ cup (160 ml) heavy cream

1 egg

4 egg yolks

2 cups (200 g) roughly chopped pecans

Preheat the oven to 350°F (180°C, or gas mark 4).

Roll out the pie crust and arrange in a deep-dish pie plate. Refrigerate until ready to use.

Combine the maple syrup, brown sugar, molasses, butter, and salt in a medium saucepan. Heat over medium heat until all of the sugar is dissolved and the butter is melted. Pour in the heavy cream and stir to combine. Let cool for 5 minutes. In a separate bowl, whisk the whole egg and egg yolks. Slowly stream the sugar mixture into the eggs, whisking to combine.

Arrange the chopped pecans in the pie crust. Pour over the sugar mixture and bake for about 1 hour, or until the center is set but just jiggles slightly. Cool to room temperature before serving.

Yield: 8 servings

CHEF'S TIP

For a chocolate pecan pie add ½ cup (90 g) dark chocolate chips in with the pecans.

MILE-HIGH CHOCOLATE CAKE
WITH PUMPKIN CUSTARD

•Soy-free

This stunning three-layer cake is made in one bowl and is so simple and delicious you will want to use it for many special occasions, or maybe even no occasion at all.

FOR PUMPKIN FILLING:

2 cups (470 ml) milk

1 can (14 ounces, or 392 g) pumpkin purée

2 eggs

4 egg yolks

1¼ cups (250 g) sugar

5 tablespoons (40 g) cornstarch

4 teaspoons pumpkin pie spice or ¼ teaspoon salt

½ cup (112 g) cold unsalted butter

1 tablespoon (15 ml) vanilla extract

FOR CAKE:

3 cups (600 g) sugar

4 cups (480 g) Liv's Flour Blend (page 15) *or 2 cups (240 g) cornstarch plus 1 cup (120 g) almond flour plus 1 cup (120 g) oat flour*

2 cups (240 g) cocoa powder

4 teaspoons baking powder

1 tablespoon (14 g) baking soda

1 teaspoon salt

6 eggs

2 cups (470 ml) milk

1½ cups (355 ml) canola oil

4 teaspoons vanilla extract

1 cup (235 ml) boiling water

3 tablespoons (22 g) powdered sugar, for garnish

To make the pumpkin filling: In a large saucepan, combine the milk, pumpkin purée, whole eggs, egg yolks, sugar, cornstarch, pumpkin pie spice, and salt. Cook over medium heat, whisking frequently, until the mixture begins to bubble. Lower the heat slightly, switch to a rubber spatula, and stir the mixture constantly until it is very thick and resembles pudding. Remove from heat. Add the cold butter and stir until completely melted. Add the vanilla and stir to combine. Pour into a heat-proof container and place plastic wrap directly on the surface to prevent a skin from forming. Cool to room temperature, then refrigerate until completely cooled and set, at least 3 to 4 hours.

To make the cake: Preheat your oven to 350°F (180°C, or gas mark 4). Grease three 8-inch (20 cm) round cake pans. Line the bottoms of the cake pans with parchment paper cut to fit, then grease the paper and set aside. (Note: If you do not have three pans, you can bake the cakes in batches.)

In a very large bowl, whisk together the sugar, flour blend, cocoa, baking powder, baking soda, and salt. Add the eggs, milk, oil, and vanilla and stir to combine. Stir in the boiling water. Distribute the batter evenly among the 3 prepared pans.

Bake the cakes for 35 to 40 minutes, or until a toothpick inserted into the center of each one comes out clean. Cool for 20 minutes, then run a sharp knife along the edge of each pan and invert each cake onto a cooling rack. Cool completely.

To assemble the cake, place 1 cake layer on a serving plate. Top with half of the pumpkin filling, then top with a second cake layer, and add the remaining filling. Top with the final cake layer. Dust with the powdered sugar before serving.

Yield: 12 servings

CHEF'S TIP

This cake recipe makes 36 cupcakes. Just fill a cupcake pan three-quarters of the way and bake for about 18 minutes at 350°F (180°C, or gas mark 4). Try using the pumpkin filling to stuff the cupcakes and top with your favorite frosting.

Christmas Cookie Exchange

SERVES 6

A cookie exchange is a great way to simplify your holiday baking. Invite several friends over, ask them to choose one cookie variety, and make a dozen for each guest attending, plus 1 additional dozen for sampling during the party. Don't forget to let them know it's a gluten-free exchange and give them copies of the recipes in this section if they need ideas! Once guests arrive, use place cards to mark each cookie variety and who contributed them. Inexpensive bakery boxes and twine make the perfect packaging for guests to bring home 1 dozen of each cookie. Put on some Christmas music, and serve hot cider or my Cinnamon Eggnog on page 88 to round out this festive, fun party.

THE MENU

Countdown to the Party Timeline

2 DAYS BEFORE:

○ Make a list and do the grocery shopping for the cookie variety or varieties you'll be making.

○ Take out all platters, serving utensils, glasses, silverware, and plates that will be needed for the party as well as any decorations or centerpieces that you will need, such as candleholders, vases, linens, etc.

○ Purchase bakery boxes and twine for guests to take cookies home in.

○ Make the dough for the cookie you've decided on, roll into a log, and store tightly wrapped in plastic wrap in the refrigerator.

○ Whisk the cocoa mix together and put them into the gift jars. Make the labels for the gift jars.

1 DAY BEFORE:

○ Prepare the marshmallows for the cocoa mix and let set. Bag them and tie to the gift jars.

○ Prepare and chill the eggnog.

THE DAY OF:

○ Bake all of the cookie dough. Place cookies on platters for serving.

1 HOUR BEFORE:

○ Light candles, put on the Christmas music, and set up an area for all of the cookies, including bakery boxes and twine. Have place cards and markers available for guests to label the cookie variety that they bring to the party.

MOM'S CHOCOLATE CHIP COOKIES

•Soy-free

My mom, Chris, made the best chocolate chip cookies when I was growing up. They were thin and crispy around the edges and chewy in the center. I spent a lot of time and effort to adapt them so they'd be just right gluten-free, and I've made her proud with these!

2 cups (350 g) semisweet chocolate chips

2 cups (240 g) Liv's Flour Blend (page 15) *or 1 cup (120 g) cornstarch plus ½ cup (60 g) almond flour plus ½ cup (60 g) oat flour*

1 teaspoon baking soda

1 teaspoon salt

½ cup (112 g) unsalted butter

¾ cup (150 g) granulated sugar

¾ cup (170 g) firmly packed dark brown sugar

1 tablespoon (15 ml) vanilla extract

2 eggs

Preheat the oven to 350°F (180°C, or gas mark 4). Line baking sheets with parchment paper and set aside.

Place the chocolate chips in a food processor and pulse to chop finely. In a medium-size bowl, mix together the flour blend, baking soda, and salt.

In a separate bowl with an electric mixer, cream the butter and granulated and brown sugars. Add the vanilla and eggs and mix until combined. Stir in the flour mixture and the chopped chocolate chips.

Drop onto the lined baking sheets by teaspoonfuls 2 inches (5 cm) apart. Bake for 9 minutes, or until the edges are crisp but the centers of the cookies still look soft. Let cool for 2 to 3 minutes before transferring to a cooling rack with a spatula.

Yield: 6 dozen cookies

CHEF'S TIP

Chopping the chocolate chips ensures that they get distributed evenly in the thin cookies. Alternatively, you could use mini chocolate chips, but reduce the measurement to 1¼ cups (220 g).

ORANGE GINGERBREAD COOKIES

•Soy-free

This recipe has the bright flavor of fresh orange to liven up an otherwise traditional gingerbread cookie. Cut these into any shapes you like using cookie cutters, bake, and leave them plain or decorate with royal icing (page 95).

¼ cup (55 g) unsalted butter, softened

¾ cup (150 g) sugar

2 teaspoons orange zest

1 egg

¼ cup (80 g) molasses

1 tablespoon (15 ml) freshly squeezed orange juice

3 cups (360 g) Liv's Flour Blend (page 15) or 1½ cups (180 g) cornstarch plus ¾ cup (90 g) almond flour plus ¾ cup (90 g) oat flour

¾ teaspoon baking powder

¼ teaspoon baking soda

1 teaspoon ground cinnamon

2 teaspoons ground ginger

¼ teaspoon freshly grated nutmeg

⅛ teaspoon ground cloves

⅛ teaspoon ground allspice

¼ teaspoon salt

Cornstarch, as needed

Preheat the oven to 350°F (180°C, or gas mark 4). Line baking sheets with parchment paper and set aside.

With an electric mixer, cream together the butter, sugar, and orange zest. Add the egg, molasses, and orange juice and mix until well combined.

In a separate bowl, whisk together the flour blend, baking powder, baking soda, cinnamon, ground ginger, grated nutmeg, cloves, allspice, and salt. Pour the flour mixture into the butter mixture and mix until well combined.

Transfer the dough to a piece of plastic wrap and pat into a disk. Wrap the dough in the plastic and refrigerate for at least 2 hours or until well chilled.

Dust a flat clean surface well with cornstarch and roll the dough out about ⅛ inch (3 mm) thick. Use cookie cutters to cut out desired shapes and transfer to the baking sheets. Dust excess cornstarch off of any scraps, knead them lightly to incorporate them, then reroll to cut more cookies.

Bake for 10 minutes, then transfer to wire racks to cool. Ice or decorate, if desired. Store in an airtight container.

Yield: 24 cookies, depending on the size and shape of your cutters

CHEF'S TIP

Cornstarch will help prevent a sticky situation when rolling out your dough. Dust the rolling surface, the top of the dough, and the rolling pin well to prevent sticking. You may need to add a bit more as you roll. Dust any excess cornstarch off of the cookies with a dry pastry brush before baking.

CHOCOLATE MONSTER COOKIES

•*Soy-free*

Monster cookies get their name for their huge size and the giant batch the
original recipe makes. Mine have cocoa added to make chocolate monster cookies,
and I've scaled down the batch to an easy-to-manage size.

3 eggs

1 jar (12 ounces, or 336 g) creamy
peanut butter

½ cup (112 g) unsalted butter,
softened

2 teaspoons vanilla extract

2 teaspoons baking soda

1¼ cups (280 g) packed light
brown sugar

1 cup (200 g) granulated sugar

½ teaspoon salt

6 tablespoons (48 g) cocoa powder

¾ cup (130 g) multicolored
chocolate candies such as M&M's

¾ cup (130 g) chocolate chips

4 cups (320 g) rolled oats

Preheat the oven to 350°F (180°C, or gas mark 4). Line baking sheets with
parchment paper.

In a very large mixing bowl, use a wooden spoon to stir together the
eggs, peanut butter, butter, vanilla, and baking soda until smooth. Add
the brown sugar, granulated sugar, salt, cocoa powder, chocolate candies,
chocolate chips, and oats. Mix well to combine.

Drop by ¼-cups (60 g) 2 inches (5 cm) apart onto the prepared
baking sheets. Flatten the dough slightly with your fingers, then bake for
9 minutes. The cookies will still look wet, but do not overbake. Let stand
for about 3 minutes before transferring to wire racks to cool.

Yield: 40 cookies

CHEF'S TIP

Be sure to use oats that are labeled "gluten-free" because oats are often
contaminated by gluten during processing.

CRANBERRY SEVEN−LAYER BARS

A festive take on the classic cookie bar, this recipe has an easy pecan shortbread crust instead of a graham cracker crust and has the addition of white chocolate chips and cranberries.

1½ cups (150 g) walnuts or pecans, divided

1 cup (120 g) Liv's Flour Blend (page 15) *or* ½ cup (60 g) cornstarch plus ¼ cup (30 g) almond flour plus ¼ cup (30 g) oat flour

¼ cup (56 g) brown sugar

¼ teaspoon salt

4 tablespoons (56 g) unsalted butter, melted

1 cup (175 g) butterscotch chips

1 cup (175 g) white chocolate chips

1 cup (120 g) dried cranberries

1 can (14 ounces, or 392 g) sweetened condensed milk

1 cup (85 g) flaked coconut

Preheat the oven to 350°F (180°C, or gas mark 4). Grease a 9 x 13-inch (23 x 33 cm) baking dish and set aside.

Combine ¾ cup (75 g) of the nuts, flour blend, brown sugar, and salt in a food processor. Pulse to finely chop the nuts and combine the ingredients. Add the melted butter and pulse until combined and the mixture is crumbly. Press into the pan and bake for 5 minutes.

Remove from the oven and layer in the remaining ¾ cup (75 g) nuts, and top with the butterscotch chips, then the white chocolate chips, and then the cranberries. Pour the sweetened condensed milk over the top, and finally, sprinkle with the coconut.

Bake for 20 minutes, or until bubbly and lightly golden at the edges. Let cool for several hours to set before cutting into 24 pieces.

Yield: 24 cookie bars

CHEF'S TIP

• Get closer to the classic seven-layer bar by using semisweet chocolate chips, subbing peanuts for the pecans, and omitting the cranberries.

• Check the ingredients on your butterscotch chips to ensure they're gluten-free! I've seen one or two brands that aren't.

ROCKY ROAD POPCORN BALLS

•Soy-free

Popcorn balls are so fun to eat, and this version is sweet, salty, crunchy, and chewy thanks to the added mini marshmallows, salted nuts, and chocolate chips. These are a great alternative to a cookie if you want something a little different.

¼ cup (56 g) unsalted butter

4 cups (200 g) mini marshmallows, divided

8 cups (80 g) popped popcorn

½ cup (55 g) chopped roasted salted almonds

½ cup (88 g) mini chocolate chips

In a medium saucepan, melt the butter over medium-low heat. Add 3¼ cups (165 g) of the marshmallows and melt until smooth, stirring occasionally.

Place the popcorn in a large mixing bowl. Pour the melted marshmallow mixture over the popcorn. Add the almonds, and stir to combine. Let cool for 2 to 3 minutes. Add the mini chocolate chips and the remaining ¾ cup (35 g) mini marshmallows and stir to combine.

Wet your hands slightly and grab about ⅓ cup (20 g) of the mixture in your hands. Press it into a ball and roll it until you have a nice even shape about the size of a golf ball. Place on parchment paper to cool completely. Repeat with the remaining popcorn mixture until you have 24 popcorn balls.

Yield: 24 popcorn balls

CHEF'S TIP

Be sure to let the marshmallow/popcorn mixture cool slightly before adding the chocolate chips so they don't melt!

CHOCOLATE SANDWICH COOKIES

•*Soy-free*

**These super chocolaty sandwich cookies with cream filling are perfect
for dunking into a cold glass of milk.**

FOR CHOCOLATE COOKIES:

1 cup (200 g) granulated sugar

6 tablespoons (84 g) unsalted butter

1 large egg

1 cup (120 g) Liv's Flour Blend (page 15) *or ½ cup (60 g) cornstarch plus ¼ cup (30 g) almond flour plus ¼ cup (30 g) oat flour*

½ cup (60 g) cocoa

¼ teaspoon salt

Cornstarch, as needed

FOR CREAM FILLING:

6 tablespoons (84 g) unsalted butter, softened

2 cups (240 g) powdered sugar

1½ teaspoons water

¾ teaspoon vanilla extract

Preheat the oven to 350°F (180°C, or gas mark 4). Line 3 baking sheets with parchment paper.

To make the cookies: Cream together the granulated sugar and the butter with an electric mixer. Add the egg and beat until combined.

In a separate bowl, whisk together the flour blend, cocoa, and salt. Add the flour mixture to the butter mixture and beat until incorporated, scraping down the sides of the bowl as needed.

Dust a flat clean surface lightly with cornstarch. Place the dough on top of the cornstarch and pat into a flat disk. Lightly dust the top of the dough with cornstarch, and roll the dough out to about ⅛ inch (3 mm) thick. Use a 1½-inch (3.8 cm) round cutter to cut the cookies, and place them about ½ inch (1.3 cm) apart onto the parchment-lined baking sheets. Dust excess cornstarch off of any scraps, knead them lightly to incorporate them, then reroll to cut more cookies. You should have 64 total.

Bake for 12 to 14 minutes, or until the cookies are crisp. Let them cool on the cookie sheets while you make the cream filling.

To make the cream filling: In a medium-size bowl, cream together the butter, powdered sugar, water, and vanilla with an electric mixer. You should have a stiff cream filling, but if the filling is crumbly, add a few drops of water at a time until the mixture holds together.

Spread about 1 teaspoon of cream filling onto a cookie and top with another cookie to make a sandwich. Repeat with the remaining cookies until you have 32 sandwich cookies. Store in an airtight container.

Yield: 32 sandwich cookies

CHEF'S TIP

The medicine cup on a cough syrup bottle can be used in a pinch if you don't have a round cutter that is the right size.

WALNUT SNOWBALLS

•Soy-free

These crumbly, buttery cookies are rolled in powdered sugar and look just like little snowballs, making them the perfect holiday cookie, but I like them anytime of the year!

1 cup (225 g) unsalted butter, softened

¾ cup (90 g) powdered sugar, divided

1 teaspoon almond extract

1 teaspoon vanilla extract

2 cups (240 g) Liv's Flour Blend (page 15) *or 1 cup (120 g) cornstarch plus ½ cup (60 g) almond flour plus ½ cup (60 g) oat flour*

¼ teaspoon salt

¼ cup (25 g) finely chopped walnuts

Beat the butter, ¼ cup (30 g) of the powdered sugar, almond extract, and vanilla extract until smooth. Add the flour blend, salt, and walnuts and mix until combined. Roll the dough into a log and refrigerate for 1 hour.

Preheat the oven to 375°F (190°C, or gas mark 5). Roll the dough into walnut-sized balls and bake 1 inch (2.5 cm) apart for 20 minutes, or until set and the tops crack slightly. Let cool, then roll in the remaining ½ cup (60 g) powdered sugar.

Yield: 4 dozen cookies

PEANUT BUTTER COCOA MIX GIFT JARS

•Soy-free •Dairy-free

Don't be fooled by this super simple recipe: it's perfect, without any fuss! I love to gift these jars of cocoa mix with a little bag of Fluffy Marshmallows (page 74).

2 cups (240 g) cocoa powder

2 cups (240 g) powdered sugar

2 cups (240 g) powdered peanut butter (I like PB2 brand)

Mix the cocoa, powdered sugar, and powdered peanut butter together in a bowl, then sift the ingredients into another bowl to ensure they are perfectly combined and there are no lumps.

Divide among six 8-ounce (224 g) mason jars, and attach gift tags that list all of the ingredients and these directions for making hot cocoa: "Heat 1 cup (235 ml) milk or dairy-free milk and pour into a mug. Stir in 6 tablespoons (48 g) of hot cocoa mix and enjoy!"

Yield: Six 8-ounce (224 g) jars

CHEF'S TIP

Powdered peanut butter is made from roasted ground peanuts that have the oil removed, so it's low in fat. Find it near the regular peanut butter.

FLUFFY MARSHMALLOWS

•Soy-free •Dairy-free •Nut-free

Who needs corn syrup? These marshmallows are so creamy and fluffy, they put store-bought marshmallows to shame! Pair them with a jar of hot cocoa mix (page 73) and you're all set for gift-giving.

½ cup (60 g) powdered sugar

½ cup (60 g) cornstarch

1 cup (235 ml) cold water, divided

3½ envelopes (1 tablespoon, or 7 g each) unflavored gelatin

2 cups (400 g) granulated sugar

½ cup (160 g) honey

¼ teaspoon salt

2 large egg whites

1 tablespoon (15 ml) vanilla extract

In a small bowl, whisk together the powdered sugar and cornstarch. Grease the bottom and sides of a 9 x 13-inch (23 x 33 cm) baking pan and dust generously with some of the powdered sugar and cornstarch mixture.

Pour ½ cup (120 ml) of the water into a small bowl. Sprinkle the gelatin over the surface of the water, and let stand for about 5 minutes to absorb some of the water (this is called "blooming" and helps the gelatin dissolve properly later).

In a medium-size heavy-bottomed saucepan, combine the granulated sugar, honey, remaining ½ cup (120 ml) cold water, and salt over medium heat. Bring the mixture to a boil and cook until the mixture reaches 240°F (115°C) on a candy thermometer, about 10 minutes.

While the sugar mixture comes up to temperature, in the bowl of a standing electric mixer, whip the egg whites to stiff peaks.

When the sugar mixture reaches 240°F (115°C), remove the pan from the heat, add the gelatin, and stir until completely dissolved. With the mixer running at a medium-low speed, slowly stream the sugar mixture into the egg whites. Add the vanilla extract and beat on high speed until thick and tripled in volume, about 10 minutes.

Use a greased spatula to transfer the marshmallow mixture into the prepared baking pan and spread evenly. Sift about ¼ cup (30 g) of the powdered sugar and cornstarch mixture evenly over the top. Chill, uncovered, until firm, at least 2 hours.

Run a thin knife around the edges of the pan and invert onto a large cutting board. Now the marshmallows are ready to be cut. Either cut out shapes with cookie cutters or cut into cubes with a sharp knife or pizza cutter. Roll all sides of the marshmallow in more of the powdered sugar and cornstarch so that they don't stick together. Place 3 or 4 marshmallows in tightly sealed plastic bags for gifting.

Yield: 24 marshmallows

CHEF'S TIP

Cut these marshmallows into tiny bite-size pieces and use in the Rocky Road Popcorn Balls on page 71.

Christmas Dinner

SERVES 6

My family always served the big Christmas dinner on Christmas Eve, and we always had roast beef. Here, I up the ante with a beef tenderloin recipe served with a luxurious caramelized onion and fig jam. The easy dinner rolls are not to be missed: they mix up in one bowl and require no kneading or rising. Save room for the caramel-y sticky toffee pudding, and if you simply can't take another bite, enjoy the apple cake in the morning. It's perfect with coffee and will make a great addition to your breakfast table.

....

THE MENU

Countdown to the Party Timeline

2 DAYS BEFORE:

○ Make a list and do the grocery shopping.

○ Take out all platters, serving utensils, glasses, silverware, cocktail items, and plates that will be needed for the party, as well as any decorations or centerpieces, such as candleholders, vases, linens, etc.

1 DAY BEFORE:

○ Wash and cut the kale for the salad. Store in a zipper-top bag in the refrigerator.

○ Make the Caramelized Onion and Fig Jam. Store in the refrigerator.

○ Prepare the root vegetables by dicing them. Store in the refrigerator to roast later, keeping the extra sauce seperate.

○ Make the Sticky Toffee Pudding. Store in an airtight container at room temperature once cooled.

○ Make the Apple Cake with Brown Butter Glaze. Store in an airtight container at room temperature.

○ Make the Cinnamon Eggnog.

THE DAY OF:

○ Set the table or buffet and decorate as desired.

○ Take out the ingredients needed for the Pear Prosecco Cocktails, and chill the prosecco.

○ Make the Caesar salad dressing.

○ Make the Parmesan Crisps for the salad.

○ Prepare the Quinoa Gratin with Broccoli Rabe. Cover and keep refrigerated, but do not bake yet.

1 HOUR BEFORE:

○ Take the Caramelized Onion and Fig Jam out of the refrigerator to come to room temperature for serving.

○ Roast the beef tenderloin 1 hour before serving. Slice the tenderloin and place on a serving platter topped with the Caramelized Onion and Fig Jam.

○ Roast the prepared root vegetables.

○ Bake the Quinoa Gratin with Broccoli Rabe.

○ Make the Super Quick Rosemary and Garlic Dinner Rolls and serve warm as soon as possible after they come out of the oven.

○ Toss the prepared kale with the Caesar dressing and serve right away.

BEFORE SERVING DESSERT:

○ In a saucepan over medium heat, warm the extra toffee sauce to serve with the cake.

KALE CAESAR SALAD
WITH PARMESAN CRISPS

•Soy-free •Nut-free

Making your own creamy Caesar dressing is easier than you think, and it pairs beautifully with kale. Parmesan crisps make this salad extra special and give crunch in place of traditional croutons.

FOR DRESSING:

2 egg yolks

2 cloves garlic, finely minced

1 teaspoon anchovy paste or 1 anchovy fillet, mashed

1 teaspoon Dijon mustard

¾ cup (180 ml) canola oil

¼ cup (60 ml) freshly squeezed lemon juice

Salt and pepper to taste

FOR PARMESAN CRISPS:

1½ cups (150 g) finely grated Parmesan cheese

FOR SALAD:

8 cups (540 g) curly kale, tough stems removed, cut into bite-size pieces

½ cup (50 g) finely grated Parmesan cheese

To make the dressing: Place the egg yolks in a medium-size bowl and whisk gently. Add the minced garlic, anchovy paste, and Dijon mustard and whisk until thoroughly combined. Keep whisking as you begin to very slowly add the canola oil, just a few drops at a time at first, then as you see the dressing begin to thicken, you can start to add the oil faster, in a thin stream, whisking constantly. When all of the oil is incorporated you should have a thick, pale emulsion, almost like mayonnaise. Whisk in the lemon juice. Season to taste with salt and lots of freshly ground black pepper. Refrigerate the dressing until ready to use.

To make the crisps: Preheat the oven to 350°F (180°C, or gas mark 4). Line a baking sheet with parchment paper. Place ¼ cup (25 g) of the Parmesan cheese in a thin layer in a circle shape, about 4 inches (10 cm) in diameter. Make 5 more circles using ¼ cup (25 g) of the remaining Parmesan cheese each.

Bake for about 8 to 9 minutes, or until the cheese is melted and has turned golden brown. Remove from the oven and let cool on the baking sheet. Use a thin spatula to remove them from the baking sheet, but handle them carefully because they are very delicate.

To assemble the salad: In a very large bowl, toss together the kale with the desired amount of dressing. Sprinkle with the ½ cup (50 g) Parmesan cheese and toss again. Season with additional salt and pepper if desired. Divide the salad among 6 plates. Top each with a Parmesan crisp and serve.

Yield: 6 servings

CHEF'S TIP

Kale is delicious and nutritious, so it's my first choice for Caesar, but use romaine if you want a more traditional salad.

ROASTED BEEF TENDERLOIN
WITH CARAMELIZED ONION AND FIG JAM

•Soy-free •Dairy-free •Nut-free

Beef tenderloin is a moist, tender, and absolutely decadent cut of meat. Here, it is complemented by a sweet and savory onion and fig jam that just melts in your mouth.

FOR TENDERLOIN:

4-pound (1.8 kg) beef tenderloin, trimmed and tied

1 tablespoon (15 ml) olive oil

Salt and pepper to taste

FOR JAM:

2 cups (320 g) finely diced white onion

2 tablespoons (30 ml) olive oil

½ cup (160 g) fig jam

2 tablespoons (30 ml) balsamic vinegar

Salt and pepper to taste

To make the tenderloin: Preheat the oven to 400°F (200°C, or gas mark 6). Rub the beef with the olive oil, then season generously with salt and pepper. Place in a roasting pan and roast for 40 minutes to 1 hour, or until a thermometer inserted into the meat reads your ideal doneness: 130°F (54°C) for medium-rare, 140°F (60°C) for medium, or 150°F (65°C) for medium-well. Remove the roasting pan from the oven, cover loosely with foil, and let rest for 10 minutes before slicing.

To make the jam: Heat a medium-size sauté pan over medium heat. Add the diced white onion and olive oil, and cook, stirring occasionally, for about 20 minutes, or until the onions are brown and sweet and have caramelized nicely. Add the fig jam, balsamic vinegar, and some salt and pepper to taste. Continue cooking for 6 to 8 minutes, or until the mixture has thickened and the vinegar has reduced. Transfer to a bowl and let cool to room temperature.

Slice the tenderloin against the grain and place on a serving platter. Spoon the jam down the center of the tenderloin and serve.

Yield: 6 servings

CHEF'S TIP

The Caramelized Onion and Fig Jam can be made several days in advance and held in the refrigerator. Bring to room temperature before serving.

ROASTED ROOT VEGETABLES
WITH BALSAMIC GLAZE

•Soy-free •Dairy-free •Nut-free

Carrots, parsnips, beets, turnips, rutabagas—winter root vegetables all roast beautifully and taste delicious with garlic, herbs, and a touch of balsamic vinegar.

4 pounds (1.8 kg) root vegetables

1 tablespoon (15 ml) olive oil

1 sprig rosemary

1 sprig thyme

3 cloves garlic, smashed

Salt and pepper to taste

¼ cup (60 ml) balsamic vinegar

Preheat the oven to 400°F (200°C, or gas mark 6).

Peel and trim the vegetables. Cut them into ¾-inch (2 cm) pieces. Place on a rimmed baking sheet with the olive oil, rosemary, thyme, garlic, and a bit of salt and pepper; toss to combine. Roast for 45 minutes, turning occasionally. Add the balsamic vinegar, turn the vegetables to coat, and cook 30 minutes more, until the vegetables are golden brown and tender inside. The balsamic vinegar should be completely reduced and just lightly coating the vegetables. Season with a little more salt and pepper if needed. Discard the rosemary and thyme sprigs, and serve.

Yield: 6 servings

CHEF'S TIP

Root veggies come in all shapes and sizes! Cutting the vegetables into pieces that are about the same size will ensure that they all cook evenly.

QUINOA GRATIN
WITH BROCCOLI RABE

•Soy-free •Nut-free

This creamy casserole is easy to throw together in advance and bake when you need it. I love the combination of ricotta and Parmesan with the slight bitterness of the broccoli rabe.

4 cups (280 g) roughly chopped broccoli rabe

¾ cup (75 g) grated Parmesan cheese, divided

½ cup (120 ml) heavy cream

½ cup (120 ml) milk

½ cup (125 g) ricotta cheese

¼ cup (40 g) finely diced white onion

4 cloves garlic, finely minced

½ teaspoon salt

⅛ teaspoon red pepper flakes

4 cups (740 g) cooked quinoa

Preheat the oven to 400°F (200°C, or gas mark 6). Grease an 8 x 8-inch baking dish and set aside.

Bring a large pot of salted water to a boil. Blanch the broccoli rabe for 1 minute, then pour into a colander to drain. Use the back of a spoon to press out any excess water.

Combine ½ cup (50 g) of the Parmesan cheese, heavy cream, milk, ricotta, onion, garlic, salt, red pepper flakes, quinoa, and broccoli rabe in a large bowl. Transfer to the baking dish and bake for 30 minutes, or until brown and bubbly.

Yield: 6 servings

CHEF'S TIP

Regular broccoli can be substituted here if you can't find broccoli rabe.

SUPER QUICK ROSEMARY AND GARLIC DINNER ROLLS

•Soy-free

**I can't say enough about these easy one-bowl dinner rolls. These gems are soft
and bready inside and perfectly crusty outside. No one will know they
are gluten-free, just that they are heavenly!**

3 cups (360 g) Liv's Flour Blend
(page 15) *or 1⅓ cups (160 g)
cornstarch plus ⅔ cup (80 g)
almond flour plus ⅔ cup (80 g) oat
flour*

4 teaspoons (18 g) baking powder

1 teaspoon salt

6 eggs

1½ cups (355 ml) milk

2 tablespoons (3.5 g) chopped fresh
rosemary or 2 teaspoons dried

4 cloves garlic, finely minced

3 tablespoons (42 g) butter

Preheat the oven to 450°F (230°C, or gas mark 8). Place a cupcake pan
in the oven for 5 minutes to heat up.

In a large bowl, whisk together the flour blend, baking powder, and
salt. Add the eggs, milk, rosemary, and garlic and whisk until smooth.

Remove the hot cupcake pan from the oven. Cut the butter into 12
pieces and place 1 piece of butter into each cupcake space. Place back
into the oven for about 1 minute to melt the butter.

Give the batter one final whisk, in case the mixture has settled at
all. Ladle the batter evenly into the compartments of the cupcake pan
and bake for 30 minutes, or until golden brown, puffed, and a toothpick
inserted into the center of a roll comes out dry.

Yield: 12 rolls

CHEF'S TIP

Preheating the cupcake pan gives these dinner rolls their chewy, delicious
crust, so don't skip this step!

APPLE CAKE
WITH BROWN BUTTER GLAZE

•*Soy-free*

Made with fresh sliced apples, this cake has a flavor that is a cross between apple pie and coffee cake. You'll make this one again and again!

FOR CAKE:

2 cups (240) Liv's Flour Blend (page 15) *or 1 cup (120 g) cornstarch plus ½ cup (60 g) almond flour plus ½ cup (60 g) oat flour*

1 teaspoon baking soda

½ teaspoon baking powder

½ teaspoon salt

1½ teaspoons ground cinnamon

½ cup (120 ml) vegetable oil

2 eggs

1½ cups (300 g) sugar

1 tablespoon (15 ml) vanilla extract

1¼ pounds (568 g) apples, peeled, cored, and thinly sliced (about 3 apples)

FOR GLAZE:

¼ cup (55 g) unsalted butter

2 tablespoons (30 ml) milk or cream

1 cup (120 g) powdered sugar

¼ teaspoon salt

2 teaspoons vanilla extract

To make the cake: Preheat the oven to 325°F (170°C, or gas mark 3). Grease a 9-inch (23 cm) springform pan and set aside.

Combine the flour blend, baking soda, baking powder, salt, and cinnamon in a medium-size bowl. Set aside.

In a medium-size mixing bowl, combine the oil and eggs. Add the sugar and vanilla and beat with an electric mixer until smooth.

Beat the flour mixture into the egg mixture. The batter will be very stiff, like cookie dough. Gently fold in the apples. Spread the batter into the prepared pan.

Bake for 1 hour, or until a toothpick inserted into the center comes out clean. Let the cake cool on a wire rack.

To make the glaze: Place the butter in a small saucepan over medium-high heat. Cook the butter until it begins to brown and smell nutty, about 4 to 5 minutes. Immediately remove the pan from the heat to prevent burning the butter and add the milk, powdered sugar, salt, and vanilla. Whisk until smooth and creamy. Drizzle the glaze over the cooled cake.

Yield: 8 servings

CHEF'S TIP

Brown butter has a rich, nutty, and complex flavor I love, but it gets bitter if you burn it! Watch the butter carefully when browning it, and remove it from the heat as soon as it starts to brown and smell nutty.

STICKY TOFFEE PUDDING

•Soy-free

This classic British dessert isn't a pudding at all, but a moist and delicious date cake topped off with a velvety toffee sauce. Pudding, cake, whatever it is, I call it awesome!

....

FOR CAKE:

2½ cups (300 g) Liv's Flour Blend (page 15) *or 1¼ cups (150 g) cornstarch plus 10 tablespoons (75 g) almond flour plus 10 tablespoons (75 g) oat flour*

2 teaspoons baking powder

1 teaspoon ground ginger

½ teaspoon salt

1¼ cups (355 ml) water

1½ cups (270 g) chopped pitted dates

1½ teaspoons baking soda

1 cup (225 g) unsalted butter, at room temperature

¾ cup (150 g) sugar

4 large eggs

2 teaspoons vanilla extract

FOR SAUCE:

2 cups (470 ml) heavy cream

1 cup (225 g) packed dark brown sugar

¼ cup (55 g) unsalted butter

½ teaspoon salt

To make the cake: Preheat the oven to 350˚F (180˚C, or gas mark 4). Grease a 9 x 9-inch (23 x 23 cm) square baking pan and set aside.

Whisk the flour blend, baking powder, ground ginger, and salt in medium-size bowl to blend; set aside.

Combine the water, dates, and baking soda in a medium-size saucepan and bring to a boil over medium-high heat. Remove from the heat and cool for about 15 minutes. The mixture will turn black and foamy.

Using electric mixer, beat the butter and sugar together in a large bowl until light and fluffy. Beat in the eggs and vanilla. Add the flour mixture and the date mixture, and beat on medium-low until smooth. Pour the batter into the prepared pan.

Bake the cake for 45 minutes, or until a toothpick inserted into the center comes out with only some moist crumbs attached.

To make the sauce: Combine the cream, brown sugar, butter, and salt in a medium-size saucepan. Cook over medium heat for about 5 minutes, whisking occasionally, until the sauce is smooth and reduced slightly.

After the cake is baked, let it cool for 5 minutes. Invert the cake onto a platter, then prick all over with a toothpick. Pour half of the toffee sauce over the cake and let sit until completely cooled and all of the sauce is absorbed.

Cut the cake into squares and drizzle a bit of the remaining toffee sauce over each slice before serving.

Yield: 12 servings

CHEF'S TIP

The toffee sauce can be made up to 3 days in advance and reheated before serving.

CINNAMON EGGNOG

•Soy-free •Nut-free

Homemade eggnog is really easy and completely heavenly. Impress all of your holiday guests by making it from scratch this year.

4½ cups (1,058 ml) whole milk

½ cup (120 ml) heavy cream

6 egg yolks

½ cup (100 g) sugar

2 cinnamon sticks

¼ teaspoon ground cinnamon

¼ teaspoon freshly grated nutmeg

⅔ cup (160 ml) bourbon (optional)

In large saucepan over medium heat, whisk together the milk, cream, egg yolks, sugar, and cinnamon sticks. Cook until the mixture thickens enough to coat the back of a spoon, whisking constantly to prevent curdling the egg yolks. Remove from the heat and let cool. Remove the cinnamon sticks and add the ground cinnamon and freshly grated nutmeg. Stir in the bourbon. Chill before serving.

Yield: 6 servings

CHEF'S TIP

Experiment with almond, coconut, soy, or rice milk for a dairy-free version of this classic treat!

PEAR PROSECCO COCKTAIL

•Soy-free •Dairy-free •Nut-free

This delicious cocktail made with Italian sparkling wine is served with a sugar cube in the bottom of the glass, which dissolves slowly as you sip your drink, sweetening it perfectly. A touch of pear brandy adds complexity and punch!

2 teaspoons pear brandy (such as Poire William)

⅔ cup (160 ml) prosecco sparkling wine

1 sugar cube

Pour the pear brandy into a champagne flute. Pour in the prosecco, drop in the sugar cube, and serve.

Yield: 1 serving

CHEF'S TIP

Other fruit brandies would be delicious here, too. Try apple brandy (Calvados) or raspberry brandy (framboise).

3

Special Occasions

Life is full of reasons to celebrate in between those big holidays! Whether you are planning a casual dinner with good friends or the perfect evening to impress someone special, I've got menu options here that are just right.

Kid's Birthday Party

SERVES 6

This really fun menu is the perfect combo of sensible and decadent treats for your child's next big celebration. Let them munch on fruit and chocolate-glazed popcorn while they play. Make chickpea pizza crusts in advance, then offer lots of healthy toppings and low-fat cheese so kids can finish them off just the way they like it. Dessert is light-as-air vanilla cupcakes, and perfectly sweet sorbet floats, made with sparkling water instead of sugary soda.

....

THE MENU

Countdown to the Party Timeline

2 DAYS BEFORE:

○ Make a list and do the grocery shopping.

○ Take out all platters, serving utensils, glasses, silverware, and plates that will be needed for the party, as well as any decorations or centerpieces, such as linens, banners, streamers, etc.

○ Make the Chocolate-Glazed Popcorn. Store in an airtight container.

1 DAY BEFORE:

○ Make the pizza crusts and store them in the refrigerator.

○ Prepare the desired toppings and sauces for the pizzas. Store separately.

○ Prepare the Lime Yogurt Dip.

○ Make the cupcakes. Store in an airtight container at room temperature.

○ Make the icing. Store at room temperature.

THE DAY OF:

○ Set the table or buffet and decorate as desired.

○ Prepare and cut the fruit and put them on skewers.

○ Slice the lemon for the Sorbet Floats.

○ Ice the Easy Vanilla Cupcakes.

1 HOUR BEFORE:

○ Take out and set up all your pizza crusts and toppings so everything is ready when it is time to make the pizzas. Have enough sheet trays prepared as well.

○ Put the Chocolate-Glazed Popcorn in a serving bowl.

○ Place the Fruit Kebabs on a platter with a bowl of the Lime Yogurt Sauce for dipping.

○ Put the Easy Vanilla Cupcakes on a serving platter.

○ Prepare the Sorbet Floats and serve right away.

MAKE-YOUR-OWN PIZZA CRUSTS

•*Soy-free*

Make these pizza crusts in advance, then let kids top them with sauce, cheese, veggies, and cooked chicken, ham, or pepperoni.

¼ cup (60 ml) olive oil, divided

2 cups (480 g) cooked chickpeas

2 eggs

1 teaspoon salt

½ cup (50 g) grated Parmesan cheese

1 cup (120 g) Liv's Flour Blend (page 15) *or* ½ *cup (60 g) cornstarch plus ¼ cup (30 g) oat flour plus ¼ cup (30 g) almond flour*

In a food processor, combine 2 tablespoons (30 ml) of the olive oil, chickpeas, eggs, salt, Parmesan cheese, and flour blend. Process until you have a smooth dough that forms a ball. Divide into 6 even pieces and roll each piece of dough into a ball.

Heat a 10-inch (25 cm) nonstick or cast-iron skillet over medium-high heat. Place 1 teaspoon of the remaining olive oil in the pan. Spray an 8-inch (20 cm) square of parchment paper with nonstick spray. Take 1 ball of pizza dough and place in the hot pan. Place the greased parchment paper on top of the dough and use a spatula to press the dough into about a 7-inch (18 cm) circle. Remove the parchment paper, and cook for 4 to 5 minutes, or until golden and crispy on the bottom, then use a spatula to flip the crust and cook for another 4 to 5 minutes, until completely set and crispy. Remove from the heat and set aside to cool. Repeat with the remaining dough until you have 6 pizza crusts.

Let cool completely and store in large zipper-top bags in the refrigerator for up to 2 days, or freeze for several months, until ready to use.

When ready to use, preheat the oven to 375°F (190°C, or gas mark 5). Top each crust with the desired ingredients, then bake for 10 minutes, or until the crust is crisp and the cheese, if using, is melted and bubbly.

Yield: 6 pizzas

CHEF'S TIPS

• Place all of the different toppings on the table in little bowls and let the kids get creative!

• Left plain and cut into wedges, these crusts make a great flatbread for scooping up hummus or other dips and spreads.

EASY VANILLA CUPCAKES

•Soy-free

These cupcakes mix up in one bowl and are more delicious, light, and airy than any boxed gluten-free cupcake mix out there! With no foreign-sounding ingredients or preservatives, you'll feel even better about serving these cupcakes to your birthday babe!

FOR CUPCAKES:

1 cup (200 g) granulated sugar

½ teaspoon salt

1 cup (120 g) Liv's Flour Blend (page 15) or ½ cup (60 g) cornstarch plus ¼ cup (30 g) almond flour plus ¼ cup (30 g) oat flour

1 teaspoon baking powder

6 tablespoons (90 ml) water

1 tablespoon (15 ml) vanilla extract

3 eggs

½ cup (120 ml) canola oil

FOR ICING:

¾ cup (168 g) unsalted butter, softened

1 tablespoon (15 ml) vanilla extract

2 tablespoons (30 ml) water

3⅔ cups (440 g) powdered sugar

To make the cupcakes: Preheat the oven to 350˚F (180˚C, or gas mark 4). Line a cupcake pan with 12 cupcake liners.

Whisk together the sugar, salt, flour blend, and baking powder in a medium-size bowl. Add the water, vanilla, eggs, and canola oil and whisk until thoroughly combined. Divide evenly among the cupcake liners.

Bake for 22 minutes, or until a toothpick inserted into the center of a cupcake comes out clean. Let cool completely before icing the cupcakes.

To make the icing: Use an electric mixer to beat the butter, vanilla, and water together. Add the powdered sugar, 1 cup (120 g) at a time, until fully incorporated, then beat for 2 to 3 minutes longer until smooth, creamy, and fluffy.

Ice the cooled cupcakes and serve.

Yield: 12 cupcakes

CHEF'S TIPS

• Canned icing is okay, if you prefer, just watch out for gluten ingredients in some varieties!

• The recipe standard for eggs is large eggs. Be sure to use large eggs in all of your recipes, including this one, for best results.

SORBET FLOATS

•Soy-free •Dairy-free •Nut-free

These frosty floats are a healthier take on an ice cream soda. Use different sorbet flavors for yummy variations and fun color combos.

6 cups (1,410 ml) seltzer water

1½ cups (228 g) sorbet of your choice

1 lemon, sliced into 6 circles

Pour 1 cup (235 ml) seltzer into each of 6 glasses. Scoop ¼ cup (38 g) sorbet into each glass. Garnish each with a lemon wheel and serve with a straw and a spoon.

Yield: 6 servings

CHEF'S TIP

Unsweetened flavored seltzers are also good here. I like lemon-lime because it has a hint of natural flavor but no artificial sweeteners.

CHOCOLATE–GLAZED POPCORN

•Soy-free •Nut-free

This popcorn has a crunchy chocolaty glaze that doesn't melt or get messy. This recipe makes enough so that the parents standing by can nibble, too!

¼ cup (50 g) granulated sugar

¼ cup (60 g) packed brown sugar

¼ cup (80 g) honey

¼ teaspoon salt

¼ cup (30 g) cocoa powder

½ cup (112 g) unsalted butter

1 teaspoon vanilla extract

10 cups (100 g) popped popcorn

Preheat the oven to 300°F (150°C, or gas mark 2). Line 2 baking sheets with parchment paper.

In a medium saucepan over medium heat, combine the granulated sugar, brown sugar, honey, and salt. Bring to a boil, stirring occasionally, and cook for 1 to 2 minutes, or until the granules of sugar have dissolved. Remove from the heat and whisk in the cocoa, butter, and vanilla until smooth.

Drizzle the sugar mixture over the popcorn, then toss the popcorn carefully (the mixture will be very hot) until all of the popcorn kernels are evenly coated. Spread onto the parchment-lined baking sheets and bake for 30 minutes, stirring every 10 minutes to prevent the popcorn from burning. Let cool on the baking sheets, stirring occasionally to keep clumps from cooling together. Once completely cooled this can be stored in an airtight container for up to 1 week.

Yield: 10 servings

FRUIT KEBABS
WITH LIME YOGURT DIP

•Soy-free •Nut-free

Kids love snacks that they can dip! These adorable kid-size fruit skewers are delicious with tangy lime yogurt dip.

1 pint (290 g) blueberries

2 kiwi, peeled and diced

1 pint (290 g) strawberries, hulled and diced

1½ cups (345 g) plain yogurt

¼ cup (80 g) honey

1 teaspoon lime zest

2 tablespoons (30 ml) lime juice

Thread the fruit onto toothpicks, alternating a piece of each fruit to make a colorful kebab with 2 pieces of each fruit per toothpick. Continue until you have 24 mini fruit kebabs.

Make the dip by whisking the plain yogurt, honey, lime zest, and lime juice together. Divide the dip among 6 small bowls or ramekins and serve 4 skewers per child with a side of dip.

Yield: 6 servings

CHEF'S TIP
Crunched for time? Simple nonfat strawberry yogurt would be a great dip, too!

Game Night

SERVES 6

Whether you're watching the football game on Sunday afternoon or getting friends together for cards or board games, this menu is packed with fun, flavorful finger foods everyone will enjoy. Paired with one of my favorite cocktails, the Classic Vodka Gimlet, this menu may have you wishing the party would never end!

....

THE MENU

Countdown to the Party Timeline

2 DAYS BEFORE:

○ Make a list and do the grocery shopping.

○ Take out all platters, serving utensils, glasses, silverware, cocktail items, and plates that will be needed for the party, as well as any decorations or centerpieces, such as candleholders, vases, linens, etc.

○ Make the Fiery Garlic Peanuts and store in an airtight container.

1 DAY BEFORE:

○ Cut up the chicken and marinate it for the Sesame Chicken Bites.

○ Make the sauce for the Sesame Chicken Bites.

○ Make the Lentil Jalapeño Hummus and store in the refrigerator.

○ Cook the shrimp for the quesadillas and store in the refrigerator.

○ Make the Chipotle Peach Chutney and store in the refrigerator.

○ Make the Brown Butter Blondies. Once cooled, cut into pieces and store in an airtight container.

THE DAY OF:

○ Start braising the bacon for the Nachos with Braised Bacon and Chipotle Peach Chutney at least 4 hours before serving.

○ Make the Spinach and Cilantro Pesto for the quesadillas.

○ Assemble the quesadillas, wrap well with plastic, and keep in the refrigerator so that they are ready to cook.

○ Set the table or buffet and decorate as desired.

○ Take out all liquors needed for the Classic Vodka Gimlets.

○ Slice lime wedges for the Classic Vodka Gimlets.

1 HOUR BEFORE:

○ Place the Fiery Garlic Peanuts in a serving bowl.

○ Take the Lentil Jalapeño Hummus out of the refrigerator to come to room temperature before serving.

○ Warm the quesadillas in a pan one at a time to heat through, melt the cheese, and crisp the tortillas. Serve on a platter with sour cream.

○ Make the nachos and arrange them on a platter with the braised bacon and chutney for serving.

○ Cook the Sesame Chicken Bites. Warm the sauce, toss with the sauce, and serve warm.

SHRIMP QUESADILLAS
WITH SPINACH AND CILANTRO PESTO

•*Soy-free*

**Rich and flavorful pesto made with spinach and cilantro is the star of this dish.
You'll love how easy it is to make.**

FOR PESTO:

1 clove garlic, minced

¼ cup (4 g) cilantro leaves, packed

½ cup (15 g) baby spinach leaves, packed

1 tablespoon (8 g) pine nuts

2 tablespoons (12 g) grated Parmesan cheese

¼ cup (60 ml) olive oil

FOR QUESADILLAS:

12 soft corn tortillas

½ pound (227 g) cooked, peeled, deveined shrimp, chopped

¾ cup (188 g) black beans

1½ cups (172 g) shredded Cheddar cheese

1½ cups (345 g) low-fat sour cream, for serving

To make the pesto: Combine the minced garlic, cilantro, spinach, pine nuts, and Parmesan cheese in the bowl of a food processor or mini food processor. Pulse to chop all of the ingredients. Add the olive oil and pulse again, until you get a thick spread that has some texture to it; it shouldn't be completely smooth. Transfer to a bowl and cover until ready to use.

To make the quesadillas: Spread a thin layer of pesto onto 1 side of each of the tortillas. Top 6 of the tortillas with chopped cooked shrimp, black beans, and shredded cheddar cheese. Top with the other 6 corn tortillas, pesto side down.

Preheat a heavy-bottomed sauté pan or cast-iron skillet over high heat. Place 1 or 2 quesadillas in the dry pan and cook for 4 to 5 minutes per side, until crispy and the cheese is melted. Transfer to a plate, and cover to keep warm while you cook the remaining quesadillas. Once all of the quesadillas are cooked, cut each one into 4 wedges and place on a platter. Serve with the sour cream for dipping.

Yield: 6 servings

CHEF'S TIP

Buy precooked shrimp for this recipe to cut down on the prep time.

SESAME CHICKEN BITES

•Dairy-free •Nut-free

**Chunks of tender chicken are tossed in a sweet and spicy sesame sauce
that is sure to please. Thighs give you the most tender and flavorful results,
but use chicken breast instead if you like.**

FOR CHICKEN:

2 pounds (908 g) boneless skinless chicken thighs, cut into 1-inch (2.5 cm) pieces

1 tablespoon (15 ml) oyster sauce

2 cloves garlic, minced

2 teaspoons toasted sesame oil

1 teaspoon kosher salt

¼ cup (60 ml) water

1 teaspoon baking powder

6 tablespoons (48 g) cornstarch

FOR SAUCE:

¼ cup (60 ml) chicken stock

¼ cup (60 ml) oyster sauce

¼ cup (60 g) brown sugar

3 tablespoons (45 ml) sriracha sauce

2 tablespoons (16 g) cornstarch

1 tablespoon (6 g) minced ginger

2 cloves garlic, minced

1 teaspoon canola oil

1 tablespoon (15 ml) sesame oil

¼ cup (60 ml) canola oil, divided

2 tablespoons (16 g) sesame seeds

To make the chicken: In a large bowl, combine the chicken, oyster sauce, garlic, sesame oil, salt, water, baking powder, and cornstarch. Let marinate while you make the sauce.

To make the sauce: In a bowl, whisk together the chicken stock, oyster sauce, brown sugar, sriracha, and cornstarch. Set aside.

In a medium-size saucepan, sauté the ginger and garlic in the canola oil over medium heat until just golden. Add the chicken stock mixture to the saucepan and cook, stirring occasionally, until thickened and the flavors have melded, about 5 minutes. Remove from the heat. Stir in the sesame oil and set aside.

Heat 2 tablespoons (30 ml) of the canola oil in a large sauté pan over medium-high heat. Add about half of the marinated chicken pieces and let cook, without stirring, for about 3 to 4 minutes, until crisp and brown on the bottom. Use tongs to flip each piece and let cook another 3 to 4 minutes, or until cooked through and crispy and golden all over. Remove with a slotted spoon to drain on paper towels. Repeat with the remaining chicken pieces and the remaining 2 tablespoons (30 ml) oil.

Place all of the cooked chicken into a large bowl, top with the sauce, and stir gently to coat all of the chicken evenly. Sprinkle with the sesame seeds and toss again. Transfer to a serving plate and serve with toothpicks for easy grabbing!

Yield: 6 servings

CHEF'S TIP

This would make a great entrée with brown rice and stir-fried veggies!

LENTIL JALAPEÑO HUMMUS

•Soy-free •Dairy-free •Nut-free

**Move over, chickpeas! Lentils make a great hummus, too. This is a healthy dip
with the zip of jalapeño and a burst of fresh lemon and garlic.**

3 cups (705 ml) water

1 cup (192 g) green lentils

3 cloves garlic

3 tablespoons (27 g) minced seeded jalapeño

1 tablespoon (15 g) tahini

¼ cup (60 ml) freshly squeezed lemon juice

¼ cup (60 ml) extra-virgin olive oil

Salt and pepper to taste

Bring the water to a boil in a medium-size saucepan. Add the lentils and cook for about 20 to 25 minutes, or until tender. Reserve about ½ cup (120 ml) of the cooking water, then drain the lentils in a colander.

Place the garlic cloves into a food processor and pulse to chop. Add the lentils, jalapeño, tahini, lemon juice, and olive oil, and a sprinkle of salt and pepper along with 2 tablespoons (30 ml) of the reserved cooking water. Process until the mixture is smooth and creamy, adding more water, if needed, to get a smooth dip that isn't too thick. Season with more salt and pepper if needed, and serve.

Yield: 6 servings

CHEF'S TIP

I serve this with lots and lots of fresh vegetables, including cucumbers, baby carrots, broccoli, and bell pepper strips. It's also great with tortilla chips.

FIERY GARLIC PEANUTS

•Soy-free •Dairy-free

**Full of flavor and spice, these are easy to prepare and make a great salty snack.
I like other nuts like cashews in this recipe, too.**

2 cups (290 g) shelled peanuts

2 tablespoons (30 ml) lightly beaten egg white

1 teaspoon garlic powder

¾ teaspoon cayenne pepper

½ teaspoon ground cumin

½ teaspoon salt

1 tablespoon (13 g) granulated sugar

Preheat the oven to 350°F (180°C, or gas mark 4). Line a baking sheet with parchment paper.

Toss the peanuts with the egg white until completely coated. Add the garlic powder, cayenne, cumin, salt, and sugar, and stir to combine. Spread the peanuts on the parchment-lined baking sheet and bake for 10 to 12 minutes, stirring occasionally, until the peanuts are fragrant and crisp. Let cool, then store in an airtight container for up to 1 week.

Yield: 6 servings

BRAISED BACON NACHOS
WITH CHIPOTLE PEACH CHUTNEY

•Soy-free •Dairy-free •Nut-free

**Slowly braising bacon makes it tender and soft, and a spicy,
sweet chutney is the perfect finishing touch.**

FOR BACON:

1 pound (454 g) slab bacon
(unsliced bacon)

½ onion, chopped

2 cloves garlic, finely chopped

¼ cup (80 g) peach preserves

1½ cups (355 ml) chicken stock
or water

FOR CHUTNEY:

1 clove garlic, finely chopped

½ cup (160 g) peach preserves

1 chipotle chile in adobo sauce

FOR NACHOS:

1 tablespoon (15 ml) canola oil,
divided

6 soft corn tortillas, each cut
into 4 wedges

2 tablespoons (6 g) finely
chopped chives

To braise the bacon: Preheat the oven to 300°F (150°C, or gas mark 2).

Heat a medium-size oven-safe sauté pan over medium-high heat.
Brown the bacon on all sides until golden, about 3 minutes per side. Add
the onion, garlic, peach preserves, and chicken stock and cover. Place in
the oven and cook for 3 to 4 hours, or until very tender. Transfer to a plate
and let cool to room temperature.

To make the chutney: Combine the garlic, peach preserves, and
chipotle chile in a food processor or mini food processor. Pulse until all of
the ingredients are combined and the mixture is smooth. Refrigerate until
ready to use.

To make the nachos: Heat a medium-size sauté pan over medium-high
heat. Add 1 teaspoon (5 ml) of the canola oil and fry the tortilla wedges, a
few at a time, until brown and crispy on all sides. Add more oil as needed,
and repeat until all of the tortilla wedges are crispy.

Arrange the tortilla wedges on a platter. Slice the braised bacon into
24 pieces and place 1 on top of each tortilla wedge. Top each with a dollop
of the chutney and sprinkle with the chives.

Yield: 6 servings

CHEF'S TIP

Packaged tortilla chips can be used instead of homemade if you like. I like
the scoop-shaped ones—the ingredients nestle perfectly inside!

BROWN BUTTER BLONDIES

•Soy-free

These are similar to a brownie in texture but are chocolate-free. Instead, they are flavored with brown sugar and nutty brown butter, which give these blondies the rich taste of butterscotch.

6 tablespoons (84 g) unsalted butter

1 cup (225 g) packed brown sugar

¼ teaspoon salt

1 cup (120 g) Liv's Flour Blend (page 15) or ½ cup (60 g) cornstarch plus ¼ cup (30 g) almond flour plus ¼ cup (30 g) oat flour

1 cup (110 g) chopped walnuts or pecans

1 egg

2 teaspoons vanilla extract

Preheat the oven to 350°F (180°C, or gas mark 4). Line an 8 x 8-inch (20 x 20 cm) baking pan with parchment paper, grease the parchment paper, and set aside.

Place the butter in a small saucepan and cook over medium-high heat, swirling the pan occasionally, until the butter begins to brown and turns fragrant and nutty, about 5 minutes. Add the brown sugar and stir until the sugar is dissolved, about 20 more seconds. Let the mixture cool slightly.

Meanwhile, whisk together the salt, flour blend, and nuts. Add the cooled butter mixture, egg, and vanilla, and stir until thoroughly combined. Pour into the greased pan and bake for 20 to 22 minutes, until just set. Let cool completely, then lift out of the pan using the parchment paper. Cut into 12 pieces and serve.

Yield: 12 servings

CHEF'S TIP

Add chocolate chips, butterscotch chips, or crushed chocolate-covered toffee candy to make these even more indulgent!

CLASSIC VODKA GIMLET

•Soy-free •Dairy-free •Nut-free

Tart and not too sweet, a vodka gimlet is my go-to cocktail when I'm out for drinks and want to keep it simple. It is really easy to make at home, too!

3 tablespoons (45 ml) vodka of your choice

1 tablespoon (15 ml) freshly squeezed lime juice

1 teaspoon powdered sugar

1 lime wedge

Fill a cocktail shaker with ice. Add the vodka, lime juice, and powdered sugar. Shake thoroughly. Strain into a martini glass and garnish with the lime wedge.

Yield: 1 serving

CHEF'S TIP
Replace the vodka with gin for a plain old gimlet.

Impress a Date Night

SERVES 2

Ah, that all-important date when you get to have someone over for the first time and show him or her what you've got in the kitchen! Whether you are gluten-free or your date is, this menu will show you know your stuff. This impressive meal is effortless to make, so you can focus on cleaning your apartment and making your bed for the first time in months. If you're lucky, you just might be serving leftover crepes to your honey for breakfast the next morning. Enjoy!

....

THE MENU

Countdown to the Party Timeline

2 DAYS BEFORE:

○ Make a list and do the grocery shopping.

○ Make the Lemon Dijon Vinaigrette. Store in the refrigerator.

1 DAY BEFORE:

○ Slice the sweet potatoes for the Herb Baked Sweet Potato Chips. Store in a resealable plastic bag in the refrigerator.

○ Make the Crepes and the Cannoli Cream filling. Store separately in the refrigerator.

THE DAY OF:

○ Set the table and arrange flowers, if desired.

○ Wash and prep the frisée and cut the chives. Store in the refrigerator.

1 HOUR BEFORE:

○ Take the Cannoli Cream out of the refrigerator to come to room temperature.

○ Make the Herb Baked Sweet Potato Chips with the prepped sweet potatoes.

○ Slice the fennel and the tomatoes and roast 15 minutes before serving. Place the salmon in the roasting pan and roast until cooked through.

○ While the salmon is roasting, make the Lemony Sugar Snap Peas.

○ Toss the frisée with the vinaigrette and serve right away.

○ Reheat the crepes in the microwave or one at a time in a warm sauté pan, fill with the cream filling, roll, and serve.

FRISÉE
WITH LEMON DIJON VINAIGRETTE

•Soy-free •Dairy-free •Nut-free

Sometimes called curly endive, frisée is crisp, bitter lettuce that resembles curly hair. It pairs wonderfully with a light, flavorful vinaigrette like this one.

FOR VINAIGRETTE:

1 clove garlic, finely minced

1 teaspoon lemon zest

2 tablespoons (30 ml) lemon juice

2 teaspoons Dijon mustard

Salt and pepper to taste

¼ cup (60 ml) olive oil

FOR SALAD:

4 cups (220 g) frisée, stems trimmed

2 tablespoons (6 g) finely chopped chives

To make the vinaigrette: Whisk together the garlic, lemon zest, lemon juice, and Dijon mustard. Season to taste with salt and pepper. Continue to whisk as you stream in the olive oil. Whisk until the oil is fully incorporated and set aside.

To make the salad: Place the frisée in a large bowl. Toss with the desired amount of vinaigrette. Sprinkle with the chives and toss again. Divide between 2 plates and serve.

Yield: 2 servings

CHEF'S TIP

Add cooked crumbled bacon and sliced hard-boiled egg for interest if you have the extra prep time.

LEMONY SUGAR SNAP PEAS

•Soy-free •Nut-free

**Simple and fresh, these snap peas take just a few moments to cook and
have a natural crunch and sweetness I adore.**

1 teaspoon butter

8 ounces (224 g) snap peas

½ teaspoon lemon zest

1 tablespoon (15 ml) fresh lemon juice

Salt and pepper to taste

Heat a medium-size sauté pan over medium heat. Add the butter and let it melt.

Add the snap peas and cook, stirring occasionally, for about 3 minutes. Add the lemon zest, lemon juice, and salt and pepper to taste. Cook for 1 to 2 more minutes, or until the snap peas are tender but still crisp. Serve right away.

Yield: 2 servings

CHEF'S TIP

Make these snap peas right before serving. The acid from the lemon juice can turn the snap peas brownish if it sits too long.

HERB BAKED SWEET POTATO CHIPS

•Soy-free •Nut-free

**These are crispy on the edges and still soft and moist in the center.
A little garlic and fresh herbs make these perfect.**

1¼ pounds (568 g) sweet potatoes

2 tablespoons (28 g) unsalted butter, melted

2 cloves garlic, finely minced

1 tablespoon (2 g) chopped fresh herbs, such as rosemary and thyme

Salt and pepper to taste

Preheat the oven to 350°F (180°C, or gas mark 4). Line a baking sheet with parchment paper.

Cut the sweet potatoes into ⅛-inch (3 mm) slices. Place them on the prepared baking sheet. Add the melted butter and toss to coat the potatoes. Add the garlic, herbs, and some salt and pepper and toss again.

Bake for 25 minutes, or until golden brown on the edges and tender in the center.

Yield: 6 servings

CHEF'S TIP

Sweet potatoes have lots of naturally occurring sugar, which tastes delicious but can burn easily! Watch these carefully as they bake, especially the ones near the edge of the baking pan.

BAKED SALMON
WITH ROASTED TOMATOES AND FENNEL

•Soy-free •Dairy-free •Nut-free

This simple, one-pan dish is light and delicious. With the flavors of fennel, roasted tomatoes, garlic, and lemon, it's sure to impress.

FOR ROASTED VEGETABLES:

1 small bulb fennel (about 6 ounces [168 g], once trimmed from stem)

1 pint (300 g) cherry tomatoes

2 cloves garlic, roughly chopped

2 teaspoons olive oil

Salt and pepper to taste

FOR SALMON:

2 fillets (5 ounces, or 140 g each) salmon, skin and pin bones removed

2 teaspoons lemon juice

1 teaspoon olive oil

Salt and pepper to taste

To make the roasted vegetables: Preheat the oven to 450˚F (230˚C, or gas mark 8). Cut the bulb of fennel in half down the center, then use your knife to cut out the small solid core of the fennel in a "V" shape. Thinly slice the cored fennel bulb.

Place the fennel, cherry tomatoes, garlic, olive oil, and some salt and pepper on a rimmed baking sheet. Toss to combine, then roast in the oven for 20 minutes.

Take the pan out of the oven, stir the vegetables, and push them to one side of the baking sheet.

To make the salmon: Place the fillets of salmon on the baking sheet next to the roasted vegetables. Drizzle the fillets with the lemon juice and olive oil and sprinkle with salt and pepper. Place the pan back into the oven and cook for 7 to 10 more minutes, or until the fish is cooked through but still very moist. The cooking time will depend on the thickness of the fish.

Use a spatula to transfer the fish to 2 plates. Top with the roasted tomatoes and fennel. Serve.

Yield: 2 servings

CHEF'S TIP

Perfectly cooked salmon should be flaky and moist. Watch the salmon carefully to avoid overcooking.

CREPES
WITH CANNOLI CREAM

•Soy-free

You can fill these crepes with just about anything, but I love using cannoli cream filling made from ricotta cheese and chocolate chips. Delish!

....

FOR CREPES:

2 cups (240 g) Liv's Flour Blend (page 15) *or 1 cup (120 g) cornstarch plus ½ cup (60 g) almond flour plus ½ cup (60 g) oat flour*

1 tablespoon (12 g) sugar

¼ teaspoon salt

2 eggs

1 cup (235 ml) milk

3 tablespoons (42 g) unsalted butter, melted

FOR CANNOLI CREAM:

⅔ cup (167 g) ricotta cheese

1 tablespoon (15 ml) heavy cream

3 tablespoons (24 g) powdered sugar

⅛ teaspoon ground cinnamon

¼ cup (44 g) semisweet chocolate chips

To make the crepes: In a medium-size bowl, whisk together the flour blend, sugar, salt, eggs, milk, and melted butter. Your batter should be thin and smooth, like melted ice cream.

Lightly spray an 8-inch (20 cm) nonstick pan with cooking spray, then heat over medium-high heat. Pour in about ¼ cup (60 ml) batter, immediately tilting and rotating the skillet to coat the bottom. Cook the crepe until set and golden brown on the bottom, about 1 minute.

Loosen the edge of the crepe with a rubber spatula, then flip it over carefully with your fingertips and cook until just set, about 20 seconds more. Swirl the pan to loosen the crepe, then transfer it to a plate and cover with plastic wrap to keep warm. Repeat with the remaining batter to make about 12 crepes.

To make the cannoli cream: Place the ricotta, heavy cream, powdered sugar, and cinnamon in the bowl of a food processor or mini chopper and pulse until smooth. Transfer to a small bowl and stir in the chocolate chips.

Place 1 crepe on a plate and spoon in a bit of the cannoli cream. Roll and repeat to make 2 per person.

Yield: 6 servings

CHEF'S TIP

Leftover crepes can be reheated the next day, just a few seconds per side in a warm, dry sauté pan. For breakfast, I like them filled with savory scrambled eggs or sweet fresh berries.

Summertime Picnic

SERVES 6

There's nothing like a fried chicken picnic, so pack your cooler and a Frisbee and find a shady spot under a tree. This fresh summertime menu will become a new favorite with your friends and family.

THE MENU

Countdown to the Party Timeline

2 DAYS BEFORE:

○ Make a list and do the grocery shopping.

1 DAY BEFORE:

○ Make the dressing for the Rainbow Veggie Slaw.

○ Make the dressing for the Watermelon Salad with Goat Cheese.

○ Make the Cookie Dough Brownies, wrap tightly, and store in an airtight container.

○ Make the Blackberry-Limeade syrup.

○ Cut the chicken breast for the fried chicken and marinate in the buttermilk mixture.

THE DAY OF:

○ Mix the dredging mixture for the chicken and set aside.

○ Make the BLT Brown Rice Salad. Store in the refrigerator.

○ Cut the vegetables for the Rainbow Veggie Slaw and Watermelon Salad (except cheese).

○ Pack a blanket, disposable cups, plates, napkins, and utensils. Pack disinfecting hand sanitizer and wet wipes for clean hands. Pack a garbage bag to make cleanup after your picnic easy. Pack a battery-powered MP3 player or radio if you'd like to hear music while you picnic.

1 HOUR BEFORE:

○ Mix the Blackberry-Limeade syrup with sparkling water and pour into a travel container.

○ Mix the Rainbow Veggie Slaw ingredients with the dressing and pack in a travel container.

○ Mix the Watermelon Salad ingredients with the dressing. Top with the goat cheese and pack in a travel container.

○ Fry the chicken and pack in a travel container.

○ Pack the remaining food items. Off you go!

BONELESS BUTTERMILK FRIED CHICKEN

•Soy-free

Crispy and perfectly seasoned, everything fried chicken should be! I make this boneless so it's easier to serve, but use a whole chicken cut into pieces, if you prefer; just fry a bit longer to fully cook bone-in chicken.

FOR CHICKEN:

3 pounds (1,362 g) boneless, skinless chicken breast

1 cup (235 ml) buttermilk

4 eggs

1 tablespoon (15 ml) Tabasco sauce

1 tablespoon (18 g) salt

FOR DREDGING MIXTURE:

2 cups (240 g) Liv's Flour Blend (page 15) *or 1 cup (120 g) cornstarch plus ½ cup (60 g) almond flour plus ½ cup (60 g) oat flour*

¾ cup (105 g) cornmeal

3 teaspoons garlic powder

2 teaspoons paprika

¼ teaspoon cayenne

2 teaspoons salt

1 tablespoon (6 g) ground black pepper

Canola oil, for frying

To make the chicken: Cut the chicken breast into 1-inch (2.5 cm)–thick strips. Whisk together the buttermilk, eggs, Tabasco, and salt in a large bowl. Add the chicken strips, cover, and refrigerate. Marinate for at least 3 hours, up to overnight.

Pour the chicken into a colander to drain.

To make the dredging mixture: In a large, clean bowl, whisk together the flour blend, cornmeal, garlic powder, paprika, cayenne, salt, and black pepper.

One by one, dip the chicken pieces into the flour mixture and firmly press the flour onto the chicken, until evenly covered in a thick coating of the flour. Place the floured chicken strips on a plate until ready to fry. Repeat with the remaining chicken until all of the pieces are coated.

Heat a large heavy-bottomed skillet over medium heat. Fill with about 1 inch (2.5 cm) of canola oil. Use a deep-fry thermometer to heat the oil to 350°F (180°C). Place a few pieces of chicken in the pan and fry for about 5 minutes, turning as needed, until golden brown and cooked through. Drain on paper towels, and repeat with the remaining chicken until all of the chicken is fried. Add more oil as needed to maintain about 1 inch (2.5 cm) of oil in the pan and bring the oil back to temperature before frying more chicken. Serve warm or at room temperature.

Yield: 6 servings

CHEF'S TIP

The right oil temperature is key to frying success. Too low, and your chicken will come out greasy; too high, and the coating will burn and turn bitter. A thermometer helps you keep the oil at the right temperature for frying.

BLT BROWN RICE SALAD

•Soy-free •Dairy-free •Nut-free

Bacon, lettuce, and tomato are tossed with brown rice and a yummy vinaigrette to make this simple side dish. It's perfect for a picnic or a potluck.

1 cup (190 g) uncooked brown rice

1½ cups (355 ml) chicken stock or water

4 slices bacon

2 teaspoons Dijon mustard

1 teaspoon honey

3 tablespoons (45 ml) apple cider vinegar

Salt and pepper to taste

1 cup (180 g) diced tomato

1 cup (30 g) baby spinach, julienned, or 1 cup (30 g) watercress, chopped

1 clove garlic, finely minced

¼ cup (25 g) thinly sliced scallion

Place the brown rice and chicken stock in a small saucepan over medium heat. Bring to a boil, then reduce the heat to low, and cook for 30 minutes. Turn off the heat and let sit for 10 minutes, covered.

Meanwhile, cut the bacon into small cubes and cook the bacon in a small sauté pan over medium heat until crispy. Use a slotted spoon to transfer the bacon to a plate lined with paper towels to drain.

Take 2 tablespoons (30 ml) of the bacon fat from the pan and transfer to a small bowl. Whisk in the Dijon mustard, honey, and apple cider vinegar.

Transfer the brown rice to a large bowl, toss with the vinegar mixture, season to taste with salt and pepper, and let cool to room temperature.

Add the cooked bacon, tomato, spinach, garlic, and scallion to the rice mixture and toss to combine. Season with more salt and pepper, if desired, and serve at room temperature.

Yield: 6 servings

CHEF'S TIP

Aside from the benefit of whole grains, brown rice has a nice chewy texture and won't get dry if you make this in advance and refrigerate it like white rice will.

RAINBOW VEGGIE SLAW

•Soy-free •Dairy-free •Nut-free

This is quite a departure from your typical goopy mayo-drenched slaw. Fresh crisp vegetables in a rainbow of beautiful colors make a delicious and nutritious alternative to coleslaw.

5 tablespoons (75 ml) apple cider vinegar

2 tablespoons (22 g) Dijon mustard

¼ cup (80 g) honey

2 tablespoons (30 ml) olive oil

1 teaspoon celery seed

1 cup (110 g) shredded carrot

2 cups (140 g) shredded red cabbage

1 yellow bell pepper, cored and julienned

1 red bell pepper, cored and julienned

1 green apple, cored and shredded

1 (5-inch, or 12.5 cm) broccoli stem, peeled and shredded

Salt and pepper to taste

In a large bowl, whisk together the apple cider vinegar, Dijon mustard, honey, olive oil, and celery seed.

Add the carrot, red cabbage, yellow and red peppers, apple, and broccoli stem. Season with salt and pepper and toss to combine. Let sit for 20 minutes before serving to meld the flavors.

Yield: 6 servings

CHEF'S TIP

For added crunch I like to add ½ cup (75 g) crushed peanuts to my slaw. Want it even peanuttier? Add 1 tablespoon (16 g) peanut butter when you whisk the vinegar mixture.

COOKIE DOUGH BROWNIES

•*Soy-free*

Two of my sweet favorites—cookie dough and fudgy brownies—fall madly in love in this recipe. And the uncooked cookie dough is egg-free, so it is worry-free, too!

FOR BROWNIES:

6 ounces (168 g) unsweetened chocolate

½ cup (112 g) unsalted butter

1 cup (200 g) sugar

3 eggs

1 tablespoon (15 ml) vanilla extract

1 cup (120 g) Liv's Flour Blend (page 15) *or ½ cup (60 g) cornstarch plus ¼ cup (30 g) almond flour plus ¼ cup (30 g) oat flour*

1 cup (175 g) semisweet chocolate chips

FOR COOKIE DOUGH:

½ cup (112 g) unsalted butter

½ cup (112 g) light brown sugar

½ cup (100 g) granulated sugar

1 tablespoon (15 ml) vanilla extract

1 cup (120 g) Liv's Flour Blend (page 15) *or ½ cup (60 g) cornstarch plus ¼ cup (30 g) almond flour plus ¼ cup (30 g) oat flour*

1 cup (175 g) semisweet chocolate chips

Preheat the oven to 350°F (180°C, or gas mark 4). Line a 9 x 9-inch (23 x 23 cm) pan with parchment paper and grease the parchment.

To make the brownies: Melt the unsweetened chocolate and the butter in a double boiler until just melted. Remove the bowl from the heat. Add the sugar, eggs, vanilla, and flour blend, and stir until thoroughly combined. Stir in the chocolate chips.

Pour into the prepared baking pan and bake for 30 minutes. The brownies should still be soft. They will firm up to a fudgy consistency once completely cooled to room temperature.

To make the cookie dough: In the bowl of an electric mixer, cream the butter and both sugars until light and fluffy, about 3 to 5 minutes. Add the vanilla, flour blend, and chocolate chips and beat until the dough is thoroughly combined. Add one or two teaspoons of water if the dough is crumbly.

Once the brownies cool completely, gently press the cookie dough evenly on top. Refrigerate for 2 to 3 hours, or until cold and the cookie dough is set. Turn out onto a cutting board and peel off the parchment. Cut into 12 squares. Before serving allow the bars to come to room temperature.

Yield: 12 servings

CHEF'S TIP

These hold up really well in the refrigerator for up to 4 days. Just cover them tightly with plastic wrap.

WATERMELON SALAD
WITH GOAT CHEESE

•Soy-free •Nut-free

**Juicy watermelon and ripe summer tomatoes are a surprisingly perfect pair.
This may become your favorite summer salad!**

4 cups (600 g) cubed seedless watermelon

½ cup (60 g) diced cucumber

1 large tomato, diced

1 cup (55 g) rinsed and roughly chopped watercress

1 recipe Lemon Dijon Vinaigrette (page 112)

4 ounces (112 g) goat cheese, crumbled

Gently toss together the watermelon, cucumber, tomato, and watercress. Drizzle on the desired amount of vinaigrette and toss to combine. Top with the crumbled goat cheese.

Yield: 6 servings

CHEF'S TIP

Make this salad even more fun by slicing the seedless watermelon into circles, then cutting the circles into wedges. Top the wedges with the remaining ingredients and eat it like a pizza!

SPARKLING BLACKBERRY LIMEADE

•Soy-free •Dairy-free •Nut-free

**Blackberries are a quintessential summer food, and they don't get the credit they deserve!
Plump and sweet when ripe, they lend their delicious flavor and beautiful color to this drink.**

2 cups (290 g) fresh or frozen blackberries, thawed

¾ cup (90 g) powdered sugar

1 cup (235 ml) freshly squeezed lime juice

4 cups (940 ml) cold sparkling water

Place the blackberries in a food processor or mini food processor and process until liquefied. Strain the seeds from the purée by passing through a fine sieve.

Combine the blackberry purée, powdered sugar, and lime juice in a large pitcher and stir to dissolve the sugar and make a thick syrup. Add the sparkling water and stir to combine. Pour into a resealable pitcher or thermos and pack for your picnic.

Yield: 6 servings

CHEF'S TIP

I love bubbles! But make this drink with filtered still water if you prefer a limeade that isn't spritzy.

Simple South American-Inspired Dinner for Friends

SERVES 6

This menu is so much fun, you can practically hear the salsa music playing already. Crispy empanadas, a spot-on ceviche, and more delicious South American flavors make this menu better than takeout. Prepare to keep the pisco sours flowing—they are a crowd favorite!

....

THE MENU

Countdown to the Party Timeline

2 DAYS BEFORE:

○ Make a list and do the grocery shopping.

○ Take out all platters, serving utensils, glasses, silverware, and plates that will be needed for the party, as well as any decorations or centerpieces, such as candleholders, vases, linens, etc.

1 DAY BEFORE:

○ Make the Corn and Black Bean Empanadas.

○ Make the baked sweet potato for the Shrimp Ceviche. Let cool and store in the refrigerator.

○ Poach the shrimp, cool with ice water, and store in the refrigerator.

THE DAY OF:

○ Set the table, bar area, or buffet and decorate as desired.

○ Chop the plantains and set aside for roasting.

○ Make the churro dough, put in a pastry bag, and store in the refrigerator. Make the sugar and cinnamon mixture, pour into a bowl, and set aside.

1 HOUR BEFORE:

○ Organize all of the liquors and ingredients for the Pineapple Pisco Sours.

○ Make the Quinoa con Pollo and keep covered to stay warm.

○ Finish making the Shrimp Ceviche and serve right away.

○ Reheat the empanadas as guests arrive and serve right away.

○ Roast the plantains.

○ Fry the churros, dip in the sugar mixture, and serve right away.

○ While the oil for the churros heats up, make the chocolate dipping sauce.

QUINOA CON POLLO

•Soy-free •Dairy-free •Nut-free

This is my take on arroz con pollo, using the healthy superfood quinoa. Quinoa originated in the Andes of South America and was a staple ingredient in Ecuador, Peru, and Bolivia long before it became fashionable in the United States.

3 pounds (1,362 g) chicken pieces

Salt and pepper to taste

1 teaspoon olive oil

¼ cup (38 g) finely diced green bell pepper

½ cup (90 g) finely diced tomato

1 cup (160 g) finely diced onion

1½ teaspoons garlic powder

¼ teaspoon ground cumin

¼ teaspoon dried oregano

⅛ teaspoon turmeric

1½ cups (260 g) quinoa, rinsed

2 cups (470 ml) chicken stock

1 roasted red pepper, cut into thin strips

¼ cup (25 g) roughly chopped Spanish olives

Season the chicken pieces well with salt and pepper. Heat a large sauté pan over high heat. Add the olive oil and the chicken and cook for 5 to 7 minutes per side, until golden brown. Transfer the chicken to a plate and set aside.

Drain all but about 1 tablespoon (15 ml) of the drippings from the pan. Reduce the heat to medium. Add the bell pepper, tomato, and onion and cook, stirring occasionally, until the ingredients have softened and the mixture has reduced and become thick, about 5 minutes.

Stir in the garlic powder, cumin, oregano, and turmeric. Add the quinoa, chicken stock, red pepper strips, and olives and stir to combine. Add the chicken pieces back to the pan, pushing them into the quinoa mixture. Cover the pan and reduce the heat to low. Cook for 20 to 25 minutes, or until the quinoa is tender and has soaked up all of the chicken stock.

Yield: 6 servings

CHEF'S TIP

Quinoa can have a bitter taste if you don't rinse it. Look for prerinsed quinoa or place the quinoa in a fine-mesh strainer and rinse thoroughly under cold water before using.

CORN AND BLACK BEAN EMPANADAS

•*Soy-free* •*Nut-free*

Empanadas are crispy little pockets of corn dough stuffed with any number of delicious fillings. This combo features corn, black beans, poblano peppers, and cheese with the perfect seasonings. I like to have these hot and ready when guests arrive. Serve them with your favorite salsa.

FOR FILLING:

2 teaspoons olive oil

½ cup (75 g) diced poblano pepper

½ cup (80 g) diced onion

2 cloves garlic, minced

½ cup (75 g) corn kernels

½ cup (125 g) cooked black beans

1 small chipotle in adobo, finely minced, plus 1 tablespoon (15 ml) adobo sauce

Salt and pepper to taste

½ cup (60 g) shredded Cheddar or Jack cheese

2 tablespoons (2 g) chopped cilantro

FOR EMPANADAS:

2 cups (240 g) masa harina

1¼ cups (295 ml) water

½ cup (120 ml) canola oil, plus more if needed

To make the filling: Heat a medium-size saucepan over medium-high heat. Add the olive oil and sauté the poblano pepper, onion, garlic, and corn until the onion is translucent, about 5 minutes. Add the black beans and the chipotle pepper and adobo sauce. Season to taste with salt and pepper.

Let the mixture cool completely. Add the shredded cheese and cilantro and stir to combine.

To make the empanadas: Combine the masa harina and water. Stir to combine. You should have a soft, pliable dough that isn't too sticky or too stiff. Divide the dough into 16 even portions and roll each one into a ball. Cover with a damp paper towel until ready to use.

Cut two 6-inch (15 cm) rounds from a heavy-duty (freezer) zipper-top plastic bag. If you don't have a tortilla press, place one plastic round on a flat surface, place a ball of the masa mixture in the center of the plastic, and top with the other piece of plastic. Use a rolling pin to roll a flat, round, 5-inch (12.5 cm) disk. If using a tortilla press, place the dough ball sandwiched in between the plastic layers into the press, close it, and press the masa into a 5-inch (12.5 cm) flat disk.

Peel off the top sheet of plastic. Place 1 heaping tablespoon (15 g) of the filling in the center of the masa and use the bottom piece of plastic to fold the dough in half, forming a half-moon shape. Press the edges together to seal the dough around the filling. Place on a plate and repeat, filling all 16 of the empanadas.

Heat a medium-size heavy-bottomed sauté pan over medium heat. Add some of the canola oil, and pan-fry the empanadas, a few at a time, until golden and crispy on each side. Transfer to a plate lined with paper towels to drain. Repeat with the remaining oil and empanadas until they are all cooked.

Yield: 16 empanadas

CHEF'S TIP

Empanadas reheat beautifully if you want to make them a day in advance and refrigerate. Just bake them on a baking sheet at 350°F (180°C, or gas mark 4) for 10 minutes, or until they crisp up and are heated through.

SHRIMP CEVICHE

•Soy-free •Dairy-free •Nut-free

My Peruvian-style ceviche is better than any you could order in a restaurant. Just toss tender poached shrimp with seasoned lime juice known as "leche de tigre" (tiger's milk) and veggies and serve.

1 (8-ounce, or 228 g) sweet potato

1 pound (454 g) peeled, deveined shrimp

1 teaspoon finely minced ginger

1 clove garlic, finely minced

1 teaspoon finely minced hot red chile pepper

¼ cup (4 g) cilantro, chopped

¾ cup (180 ml) freshly squeezed lime juice

Salt to taste

½ cup (75 g) fresh corn kernels

½ red onion, thinly sliced

Preheat the oven to 350°F (180°C, or gas mark 4). Pierce the sweet potato with a fork and bake for 45 minutes, or until just cooked through but not mushy. Set aside to cool completely.

Meanwhile, cook the shrimp. Fill a large stockpot with cold water and enough salt to make it taste like seawater. Cover and bring to a boil. Fill a large mixing bowl with ice and water. Add the shrimp to the boiling water and allow to cook for 3 minutes, or until just cooked through. Pour the shrimp into a colander to drain and add the shrimp to the cold ice water to stop the cooking and cool the shrimp. Drain again. Place in a large bowl.

Make the leche de tigre by combining the ginger, garlic, minced chile, cilantro, and lime juice. Season with salt and pour the mixture over the shrimp.

Peel the baked sweet potato and cut it into ¾-inch (2 cm) cubes. Add to the shrimp mixture. Add the fresh corn and the red onion and toss to combine. Serve right away.

CHEF'S TIP

Serve with tortilla chips to scoop up the ceviche if you'd like.

OVEN–ROASTED SWEET PLANTAINS

•Soy-free •Dairy-free •Nut-free

Roasting plantains instead of frying them makes them healthier and frees up space on your stove so that you can tend to the other dishes you're making.

2½ pounds (1,135 g) very ripe plantains

1 tablespoon (15 ml) olive oil

2 tablespoons (24 g) sugar

Salt to taste

Preheat the oven to 400°F (200°C, or gas mark 6). Line a baking sheet with aluminum foil and set aside.

Peel the plantains and cut into 1-inch (2.5 cm)–thick slices. Place them in a bowl and toss with the olive oil. Add the sugar and a sprinkle of salt, and toss again.

Place in the center of the aluminum foil, bring the edges around, and wrap the plantains in foil. Bake for 20 minutes.

Open the foil, spread the plantains out, and place under the broiler for 1 minute to lightly brown the edges. Serve warm.

Yield: 6 servings

CHEF'S TIP

Like bananas, plantains are often green or yellow in the store. For optimum sweetness, be sure to buy these about a week early so that they have a chance to fully ripen and turn mostly black before you use them.

PINEAPPLE PISCO SOURS

•Soy-free •Dairy-free •Nut-free

Pisco is a grape brandy made in Peru or Chile. Traditionally made with lime juice, this drink tastes similar to a margarita because it's tart and sweet, but here, pineapple juice adds a fun twist. A pisco sour is made frothy with an egg white.

½ cup (120 ml) pisco

3 tablespoons (44 ml) pineapple juice

1 tablespoon (15 ml) freshly squeezed lime juice

2 tablespoons (16 g) powdered sugar

1 egg white

3 dashes angostura bitters

Fill a cocktail shaker with ice. Add the pisco, pineapple juice, lime juice, sugar, egg white, and 1 dash of bitters to the shaker. Shake thoroughly. Strain into 2 glasses. Add 1 dash of bitters to each glass to mark the froth in the glass with a reddish tint.

Yield: 2 servings

CHEF'S TIP

Raw eggs are generally very safe thanks to their natural protective coating—the shell! If you feel more comfortable using pasteurized egg whites in a carton, 3 tablespoons (45 ml) pasteurized egg whites can be substituted for 1 egg white.

CINNAMON CHURROS
WITH CHOCOLATE SAUCE

•*Soy-free*

Churros are chewy, fried donut sticks rolled in cinnamon sugar. Want to send your guests home in a state of bliss? Just add chocolate sauce.

FOR COATING:

⅓ cup (67 g) sugar

1 teaspoon ground cinnamon

FOR CHURROS:

¾ cup (180 ml) water

2 tablespoons (30 ml) canola oil, plus more for frying

¼ teaspoon salt

2 tablespoons (24 g) sugar

1 cup (120 g) Liv's Flour Blend (page 15) *or ½ cup (60 g) cornstarch plus ¼ cup (30 g) almond flour plus ¼ cup (30 g) oat flour*

1 egg

1 tablespoon (15 ml) vanilla extract

FOR CHOCOLATE SAUCE:

¼ cup (60 ml) milk

1 teaspoon butter

½ cup (88 g) dark chocolate chips or chopped dark chocolate

¼ teaspoon vanilla extract

To make the coating: Combine the sugar and cinnamon in a shallow bowl and set aside.

To make the churros: Bring the water and 2 tablespoons (30 ml) canola oil to a boil.

In a small bowl, combine the salt, sugar, and flour blend. Pour the mixture into the boiling water and, stirring constantly with a wooden spoon, cook over medium heat for about 1 minute, until the mixture forms a thick ball of dough.

Place the dough in a bowl and beat with an electric mixer for 1 minute to cool the mixture slightly. Add the egg and vanilla and beat until thoroughly combined. The dough should be stiff. Place the dough in a sturdy pastry bag fitted with a #4 star tip.

Place about 1 inch (2.5 cm) of canola oil in a small saucepan or frying pan. Heat the oil to 350°F (180°C) on a deep-fry thermometer. Pipe 5-inch (12.5 cm) lengths of dough directly into the hot oil, using clean scissors to cut the dough, releasing it into the oil. Working quickly, repeat until you have 4 or 5 churros piped into the oil. Cook the churros, flipping once, until they are golden and cooked through, about 2 to 3 minutes. Drain the churros on paper towels, then roll them in the prepared cinnamon-sugar coating.

Repeat until you've used all the dough, being careful to keep the oil at 350°F (180°C) and adding more oil to your pan if needed.

To make the chocolate sauce: Bring the milk and butter to a boil in a small saucepan. Add the dark chocolate and vanilla and stir until the chocolate is melted and the mixture is smooth. Serve the churros with the chocolate sauce on the side for dipping.

Yield: 6 servings

CHEF'S TIP

These are best served warm right after you've prepared them. The churros tend to get soggy if prepped too far in advance.

Baby Shower Brunch Buffet

SERVES 6

Baby on board! This really fun brunch menu is easily doubled or tripled to accommodate all of your special guests. The perfect buttermilk biscuits are the foundation for a beautiful buffet full of toppings and spreads for your biscuits. Whether you or your guest of honor is gluten-free, everyone in attendance will enjoy this menu!

THE MENU

Countdown to the Party Timeline

2 DAYS BEFORE:

○ Make a list and do the grocery shopping.

○ Take out all platters, serving utensils, glasses, silverware, and plates that will be needed for the party, as well as any decorations or centerpieces, such as candleholders, vases, linens, etc.

○ Whisk together the dry ingredients for the Buttermilk Biscuits. Store in a zipper-top bag.

○ Make the Honey Butter, Strawberry Cream Cheese, and Chocolate Cashew Spread, and store in the refrigerator.

○ Prepare the Sugar and Spice Cookie Mix Party Favors.

1 DAY BEFORE:

○ Set the table, bar area, or buffet and decorate as desired.

THE DAY OF:

○ Make the Baked Veggie and Egg Patties.

○ Make the Crispy Baked Hash Browns.

○ Make the Morning Sunrise Mocktail.

1 HOUR BEFORE:

○ Finish making the Buttermilk Biscuits, and bake. Serve warm.

○ Make the Maple-Glazed Bacon with Cracked Black Pepper.

○ Reheat the hash browns before serving.

○ Make the Quick Sausage Gravy.

BUTTERMILK BISCUITS

•Soy-free •Dairy-free

Because these biscuits are the star of your baby shower brunch buffet, I knew I had to get them perfect. Buttery and rich, with the most beautiful crumb, they're a great base for all of the beautiful sauces and spreads on this menu.

4 cups (480 g) Liv's Flour Blend (page 15) *or 2 cups (240 g) cornstarch plus 1 cup (120 g) almond flour plus 1 cup (120 g) oat flour, plus more for rolling*

2 tablespoons (24 g) sugar

1 tablespoon (14 g) baking powder

1 teaspoon baking soda

1½ teaspoons salt

1½ cups (336 g) cold unsalted butter, cut into ½-inch (1.3 cm) cubes

1 to 1¼ cups (235 to 295 ml) well-shaken buttermilk

1 egg, beaten

Preheat the oven to 400°F (200°C, or gas mark 6). Line baking sheets with parchment paper and set aside.

In the bowl of a food processor, combine the flour blend, sugar, baking powder, baking soda, and salt. Pulse to combine.

Add the cold butter and pulse until it is in pea-size pieces, evenly distributed throughout the flour. Add about ¾ cup (180 ml) of the buttermilk and pulse. The dough should just begin to hold together. If it's dry, add about 2 tablespoons (30 ml) more buttermilk at a time and pulse again, repeating as needed until the dough begins to hold together

Turn out the dough onto a clean flat surface, dusted lightly with oat flour. Knead the dough two or three times to bring the dough together, and then roll out the dough into a 1½-inch (3.8 cm)-thick square that is about 9 x 9 inches (23 x 23 cm). Use a sharp knife dusted with cornstarch to cut the biscuits into 16 squares. Place the biscuits 3 inches (7.5 cm) apart on the baking sheet.

Use a dry pastry brush to dust off any excess cornstarch from the biscuits, then brush the biscuits with the beaten egg, and bake for 12 to 14 minutes, or until golden.

Yield: 16 biscuits

CHEF'S TIPS

• To make this recipe egg-free, brush the tops of the biscuits with melted butter instead of the beaten egg.
• These biscuits go great with any of the spreads from page 142.

SPREADS

These delicious spreads are perfect with the Buttermilk Biscuits (all pictured on page 141) and take under 5 minutes to prepare. Make just one, or try them all and let your guests choose!

....

STRAWBERRY CREAM CHEESE

•Soy-free •Nut-free

½ cup (75 g) diced strawberries

1 cup (230 g) cream cheese, softened

2 tablespoons (16 g) powdered sugar

Place the strawberries in a bowl and lightly mash them with a fork. Add the softened cream cheese and powdered sugar, and stir to combine. Refrigerate until ready to serve.

Yield: 12 servings

CHOCOLATE CASHEW SPREAD

•Soy-free •Dairy-free

⅔ cup (170 g) cashew butter

¼ cup (60 ml) warm water

2 tablespoons (16 g) cocoa powder

2 tablespoons (16 g) powdered sugar

Whisk together the cashew butter, warm water, cocoa powder, and powdered sugar until well blended. Refrigerate to store, then serve at room temperature.

Yield: 12 servings

HONEY BUTTER

•Soy-free •Nut-free

½ cup (112 g) unsalted butter, softened

¼ cup (80 g) honey

¼ teaspoon salt

Stir together the butter, honey, and salt until well combined. Refrigerate until ready to serve.

Yield: 12 servings

QUICK SAUSAGE GRAVY

•Soy-free •Nut-free

I never had sausage gravy until I moved to South Carolina for my first job out of culinary school. Now, biscuits seem naked without a creamy spoonful of this milk-based gravy on top. The secret is to use lots of freshly ground black pepper for the right flavor.

½ pound (228 g) breakfast sausage meat, no casing

3 tablespoons (24 g) cornstarch

2 cups (470 ml) milk

Salt and coarsely ground black pepper to taste

In a medium-size saucepan over medium-high heat, brown the breakfast sausage. Drain any excess fat, then put the sausage back into the saucepan.

Sprinkle the meat with the cornstarch, and stir to coat evenly. Lower the heat to medium, add the milk, and stir. Cook for 6 to 7 minutes, stirring occasionally, until it comes to a boil and thickens.

Season with salt and lots of cracked black pepper. Serve warm.

Yield: 6 servings

CHEF'S TIP

Adjust the knob on the top of your pepper mill to adjust the grind of the pepper. Turn the knob tighter for a finer grind, and loosen for a coarse grind.

BAKED VEGGIE AND EGG PATTIES

•Soy-free •Dairy-free •Nut-free

Baking the eggs into patties makes them easy to serve and perfect for sandwiching between biscuits.

1 teaspoon olive oil

¼ cup (40 g) diced white onion

¼ cup (38 g) diced red pepper

¼ cup (38 g) diced green pepper

¼ teaspoon plus a pinch salt, divided

¼ teaspoon plus a pinch freshly ground black pepper, divided

6 eggs

Preheat the oven to 350°F (180°C, or gas mark 4). Spray 6 compartments in a cupcake pan with nonstick cooking spray and set aside.

Heat a medium-size sauté pan over medium heat. Add the olive oil and sauté the onion, red pepper, and green pepper until soft, about 5 to 7 minutes. Season with a pinch each of the salt and pepper. Distribute the mixture evenly among the 6 greased cupcake compartments.

Crack the 6 eggs into a large bowl. Beat together with the remaining ¼ teaspoon salt and remaining ¼ teaspoon pepper. Divide the beaten eggs among the 6 greased cupcake compartments.

Bake for 15 to 20 minutes, or until the eggs are completely set in the center. Remove from the oven and let cool for 1 to 2 minutes before carefully unmolding and serving.

Yield: 6 servings

CRISPY BAKED HASH BROWNS

•Soy-free •Nut-free

**Potatoes and cheese bake up into crispy, savory hash browns so good,
and so easy, that you'll never want to fry them again.**

2 medium-size russet potatoes, peeled and coarsely grated (about 1¼ pounds [568 g])

2 cloves garlic, minced

½ cup (60 g) shredded Cheddar or Swiss cheese

2 tablespoons (8 g) chopped parsley

2 tablespoons (16 g) cornstarch

1 teaspoon salt

½ teaspoon onion powder

½ teaspoon garlic powder

½ teaspoon paprika

Preheat the oven to 350°F (175°C, or gas mark 4). Line 2 baking sheets with parchment paper and spray the paper generously with nonstick spray.

Place a colander in your sink and place the shredded potatoes into the colander. Drain any excess liquid from the potatoes by pushing down on the potatoes and letting the liquid drain down the sink. Place the potatoes in a large bowl.

Add the minced garlic, shredded cheese, chopped parsley, cornstarch, salt, onion powder, garlic powder, and paprika and stir to combine.

Make 6 mounds of the potato mixture, spaced evenly, on each baking sheet to make a total of 12 hash browns. Press down on the potatoes to flatten each mound into a flat, round shape. Spray lightly with nonstick spray and place in the oven to bake. Cook for about 20 minutes, then flip with a spatula and cook another 10 to 15 minutes, or until evenly browned and crispy.

Yield: 6 servings

CHEF'S TIP

Try a mixture of half russet and half sweet potato for a sweet variation.

MAPLE–GLAZED BACON
WITH CRACKED BLACK PEPPER

•Soy-free •Dairy-free •Nut-free

I slather melt-in-your-mouth thick-cut bacon with sweet maple syrup and crust it with coarsely ground black pepper for an over-the-top twist on this breakfast staple.

2 pounds (908 g) thick-cut bacon

6 tablespoons (90 ml) maple syrup

1 tablespoon (6 g) cracked black pepper, or more to taste

Preheat the oven to 350˚F (180˚C, or gas mark 4). Line a rimmed baking sheet with parchment paper. Place the bacon in a single layer on the parchment and bake for about 15 minutes.

Flip the bacon and rearrange for even cooking (pieces on the outside tend to brown faster than the bacon pieces in the center of the baking sheet). Use a pastry brush to brush the bacon with the maple syrup, then sprinkle with the cracked pepper. Bake an additional 10 to 15 minutes, or until brown and crispy. Transfer to paper towels to drain, then serve.

Yield: 6 servings

CHEF'S TIP

If any pieces of bacon begin to get too brown before the others are done, remove them to a plate while the others finish cooking.

SUGAR AND SPICE COOKIE MIX PARTY FAVORS

•Soy-free •Dairy-free •Nut-free

Sugar and spice and everything nice! These cinnamon oatmeal chocolate chip cookies are great edible favors and are free from major allergens. Use pink or blue M&M's depending on whether your mommy-of-honor is expecting a boy or girl.

1⅓ cups (160 g) Liv's Flour Blend (page 15) *or ⅔ cup (80 g) cornstarch plus ⅓ cup (40 g) almond flour plus ⅓ cup (40 g) oat flour*

¾ cup (60 g) rolled oats

½ cup (112 g) packed brown sugar

½ cup (100 g) granulated sugar

¾ cup (130 g) candy-coated chocolate pieces such as M&M's

¾ cup (130 g) semisweet chocolate chips

1 teaspoon baking powder

1 teaspoon baking soda

1 teaspoon cinnamon

¼ teaspoon salt

Layer the ingredients in a 1-quart (1 liter) mason jar in the order given. Level each layer by tapping the jar before adding the next layer.

Include a card or label with the following instructions: *Preheat the oven to 350˚F (180˚C, or gas mark 4). Line baking sheets with parchment paper. In a medium bowl, mix together ½ cup (112 g) melted butter or margarine, 1 egg, and 1 teaspoon vanilla extract. Stir in the entire contents of the jar using a wooded spoon. Drop by tablespoonfuls 2 inches (5 cm) apart onto the prepared baking sheets. Bake for 9 minutes. Transfer to wire racks to cool. Makes 36 cookies.*

Yield: 1 party favor

CHEF'S TIP

You'll most likely be making a bunch of these at once. Lay out the jars on your counter and measure one ingredient at a time into each jar, assembly line style.

MORNING SUNRISE MOCKTAIL

•Soy-free •Dairy-free •Nut-free

This pretty drink is a take on the virgin tequila sunrise, except mine is made with homemade pomegranate syrup instead of bottled grenadine.

FOR POMEGRANATE SYRUP:

½ cup (120 ml) pomegranate juice such as POM

½ cup (100 g) sugar

FOR COCKTAIL:

1 tablespoon (15 ml) pomegranate syrup

½ cup (120 ml) chilled pineapple juice

½ cup (120 ml) chilled orange juice

1 orange slice

To make the syrup: Pour the pomegranate juice and sugar into a small saucepan. Heat over medium heat until the sugar is completely dissolved. Let cool.

To make the cocktail: Place 1 tablespoon (15 ml) of the pomegranate syrup into the bottom of a glass. Gently layer the pineapple and orange juices in the glass and serve garnished with the orange slice.

Yield: 1 serving

Spanish Tapas-Style Dinner Party

SERVES 6

Tapas are small dishes meant to be enjoyed with wine or sangria. They can range from a simple bowl of olives to more hearty, protein-heavy dishes. For this dinner party, I've included my favorite tapas dishes, all done simply and deliciously gluten-free with authentic flavors like sherry, smoked paprika, and garlic. In the timeline, I'll show you when to prep everything to keep the tapas flowing without keeping you tied to the stove. Each recipe makes enough for 6 tapas-size portions, but this menu can be easily doubled for a bigger crowd.

THE MENU

Countdown to the Party Timeline

2 DAYS BEFORE:

○ Do the grocery shopping.

○ Plan the table setting, including linens, centerpieces, etc.

○ Have all the serving platters and serving utensils you will need ready for each dish.

1 DAY BEFORE:

○ Make the coconut flan and chill.

○ Make the Lamb Meatballs in Tomato Sauce. Let cool and store tightly covered in the refrigerator. These can easily be heated up right before serving.

○ Make the Almond Saffron Chicken. Let cool and store tightly covered in the refrigerator. This can easily be heated up right before serving.

○ If you are using frozen shrimp for the Garlic Shrimp, defrost them in the refrigerator overnight.

○ Boil the potatoes for the Potato Tortilla, let cool, and store whole in the refrigerator.

○ Prepare the Smoked Paprika Aioli for the Potato Tortilla. Store tightly covered in the refrigerator until ready to use.

○ Set the scene for your party. Arrange flowers, if using, and set the table for the party.

THE DAY OF:

○ Make and chill the Red Sangria.

○ Slice the shrimp in half and put back into the refrigerator until ready to cook.

○ Prepare the brussels sprouts for the Roasted Brussels Sprouts with Chorizo by cleaning and slicing them in half. Slice the chorizo and put both back in the refrigerator.

○ Make the Marinated Olives.

○ Make the Manchego with Membrillo and Honey.

○ Slice the boiled potatoes, and make the tortilla. Once the tortilla is done, cover with foil (this can be served warm or at room temperature).

1 HOUR BEFORE:

○ Put out the Marinated Olives and the Manchego with Membrillo and Honey.

○ Heat up the Lamb Meatballs in Tomato Sauce and the Almond Saffron Chicken in sauté pans or in the oven at 375°F (190°C, or gas mark 5) until hot.

○ Toss the brussels sprouts, chorizo, oil, and salt together and roast in the oven.

○ Make the Blistered Shishito Peppers.

○ Make the Garlic Shrimp.

MARINATED OLIVES

•Soy-free •Dairy-free •Nut-free

Simple recipes are often the most delicious. Here, a few ingredients quickly perk up your average olive. These are really special (pictured on page 154)!

2 cups (200 g) assorted olives

3 cloves garlic, finely minced

1 tablespoon (4 g) chopped parsley

½ teaspoon crushed red pepper flakes

1 sprig rosemary, needles removed from the stem and roughly chopped

½ lemon, peel and all, chopped into ½-inch (1.3 cm) pieces

Combine all of the ingredients in a bowl and marinate overnight. Serve with toothpicks for picking up the olives and a small bowl on the side for discarding pits if your olives are not pitted.

MANCHEGO
WITH MEMBRILLO AND HONEY

•Soy-free •Nut-free

Membrillo is a thick sliceable red fruit paste made from quince. It's the classic pairing for Spanish Manchego, a hard, mild sheep's milk cheese. Look for it where you find your specialty cheeses.

8 ounces (227 g) membrillo (quince paste)

8 ounces (227 g) Manchego cheese

1 tablespoon (20 g) honey

Dice the membrillo and Manchego into ½-inch (1.3 cm) cubes. Thread 1 piece of cheese and 1 piece of membrillo onto toothpicks. Drizzle with the honey and serve.

Yield: 6 servings

CHEF'S TIP
Cheeses are best served at room temperature rather than cold. Let this sit out for about 20 minutes before drizzling with honey, then serve.

POTATO TORTILLA
WITH SMOKED PAPRIKA AIOLI

•Soy-free •Dairy-free •Nut-free

**Sometimes called a Spanish omelet, a potato tortilla is one of the most popular
and traditional tapas dishes. The rich, smoked paprika aioli is optional, but it is so good,
I wouldn't skip it! Serve this dish hot or at room temperature.**

FOR TORTILLA:

2 pounds (908 g) waxy potatoes such as Yukon gold potatoes, peeled

7 eggs

2 teaspoons salt

¼ teaspoon black pepper

1 tablespoon (15 ml) olive oil

½ onion, thinly sliced

FOR AIOLI:

2 egg yolks

¾ cup (180 ml) canola oil

4 teaspoons lemon juice

1 teaspoon smoked paprika

Salt and pepper to taste

Preheat the oven to 375°F (190°C, or gas mark 5).

To make the tortilla: Place the potatoes in cold water and cover, bring to a boil, and boil the potatoes until just tender. Drain, let cool, and then slice thinly into ⅛-inch (3 mm) slices.

Whisk together the eggs, salt, and pepper. Heat the olive oil in a 10-inch (25 cm) oven-safe sauté pan or cast-iron skillet over medium-high heat. Alternate layers of the potatoes and thinly sliced onion in the pan. Pour the beaten eggs over the potatoes, and press down on the potatoes to evenly distribute the egg. Let cook for 1 to 2 minutes, or until the egg along the edge of the pan begins to set. Transfer the pan to the oven and bake for 25 minutes, or until the egg is completely set.

To make the aioli: Whisk the egg yolks in a heavy, medium-size bowl until thick, about 1 minute. Very slowly, begin to drizzle in a few drops of the canola oil, whisking as you go. The mixture should begin to thicken as you add the oil. Keep whisking and adding the canola oil in a very slow stream until all of the oil is incorporated into the egg yolks and the mixture is thick and creamy. Add the lemon juice, paprika, and salt and pepper to taste. Refrigerate until ready to use.

When the tortilla is finished cooking, remove it from the oven and let cool for 5 minutes (this will make it easier to remove from the pan), then run a spatula along the edge of the tortilla to loosen it from the pan. Place a serving plate on top of the tortilla, then invert the tortilla so that the plate is now on the bottom and you can remove the pan from the top.

Slice the tortilla into wedges (I like to cut it into 12 and let guests go back for seconds, if desired) and serve with the aioli on the side.

Yield: 6 servings

CHEF'S TIP

Try the lazy man's version of this recipe by using 5 cups (about 6 ounces [168 g]) lightly salted store-bought potato chips in place of the cooked potatoes. Lightly crush them, combine them with the egg, onion, and black pepper (omit the salt!), and pour into the hot skillet coated with olive oil. It comes together in moments!

BLISTERED SHISHITO PEPPERS

•Soy-free •Dairy-free •Nut-free

I love when a simple preparation highlights a food's natural deliciousness, and it doesn't get simpler than this. Blistered peppers are my friends' favorite tapas dish. They disappear in moments every time!

1 tablespoon (15 ml) olive oil

1 pound (454 g) whole shishito peppers

Kosher salt or sea salt, to taste

Heat a large heavy-bottomed sauté pan over medium heat. Add the olive oil and shishito peppers and cook, stirring occasionally, for about 3 to 4 minutes, or until the skins of the peppers are blistered and the peppers are just softened but not mushy.

Sprinkle generously with salt and serve with a small bowl on the side to discard the stems after eating.

Yield: 6 servings

CHEF'S TIP

Any small and mildly spicy pepper will do here. Padrón peppers are another good option, if you can find them.

ROASTED BRUSSELS SPROUTS
WITH CHORIZO

•Soy-free •Dairy-free •Nut-free

Simple and foolproof, this savory recipe will soon become a favorite!

1 pound (454 g) brussels sprouts

6 ounces (168 g) cured Spanish chorizo

1 teaspoon olive oil

Salt and pepper to taste

Preheat the oven to 400°F (200°C, or gas mark 6).

Trim the brown ends off of the stems of the brussels sprouts and cut them in half. Place them on a baking sheet. Slice the chorizo into thin slices and place them on the baking sheet as well. Drizzle the brussels sprouts and chorizo with the olive oil, season with salt and pepper, and toss to combine.

Spread everything out in an even layer on the baking sheet and bake for 15 minutes, turning once or twice for even browning. The brussels sprouts should be tender but not mushy and have some charred leaves on the outside, while the chorizo will be browned and slightly crisp.

Yield: 6 servings

GARLIC SHRIMP
(GAMBAS AL AJILLAS)

•Soy-free •Dairy-free •Nut-free

This easy dish takes just a few minutes to prepare and should be made right before serving. Don't be shy about using all ten cloves of garlic; with the combination of smoked paprika, sherry, and a touch of lemon, this recipe is just right!

10 cloves garlic

1 pound (454 g) peeled, deveined shrimp

¾ teaspoon smoked paprika

Salt and pepper to taste

1 tablespoon (15 ml) olive oil

2 tablespoons (30 ml) lemon juice

½ cup (120 ml) dry sherry

1 tablespoon (4 g) chopped parsley

Roughly chop 5 cloves of the garlic. Finely grate the remaining 5 cloves on a Microplane or push through a garlic press. Set aside.

Remove the tails from the shrimp if they are still attached. Slice the shrimp in half from head to tail. Season them with the smoked paprika and a bit of salt and pepper.

Place the olive oil in a large skillet along with the 5 cloves of garlic that are roughly chopped. Turn on the heat and set it at medium-high. When the garlic begins to sizzle and just starts to turn golden at the edges, add the shrimp and the finely grated garlic. Sauté for about 4 minutes, or until the shrimp curl and turn pink. Turn the heat up to high, add the lemon juice and sherry, and cook for 2 to 3 more minutes, until the shrimp are fully cooked and the sauce is reduced slightly. Turn off the heat, toss with the parsley, and serve.

Yield: 6 servings

CHEF'S TIP

Cutting the shrimp in half makes them curl into beautiful spirals as they cook.

LAMB MEATBALLS IN TOMATO SAUCE

•Soy-free •Dairy-free •Nut-free

These meatballs are perfect tapas fare because they're sized for nibbling. Instead of breadcrumbs they are bound with cooked rice, making them naturally gluten-free. Use leftover rice if you have some on hand.

FOR MEATBALLS:

1 egg

½ cup (80 g) cooked white or brown rice

1 pound (454 g) ground lamb

4 cloves garlic, finely minced

¼ cup (16 g) parsley, finely chopped

¼ teaspoon ground cumin

¼ teaspoon ground coriander

¼ teaspoon garlic powder

½ teaspoon salt

¼ teaspoon black pepper

FOR SAUCE:

¼ cup (40 g) finely diced white onion

¼ cup (38 g) finely diced green bell pepper

2 cloves garlic, minced

½ cup (120 ml) dry sherry

1½ cups (270 g) crushed tomatoes

¼ teaspoon smoked paprika

Salt and pepper to taste

To make the meatballs: In the bowl of a food processor or mini food processor, combine the egg and rice. Pulse until the mixture is smooth. Combine it with the lamb, fresh garlic, parsley, cumin, coriander, garlic powder, salt, and pepper in a medium-size bowl. Use wet hands to form the mixture into 24 small balls.

Heat a large sauté pan over medium-high heat. Brown the meatballs, turning occasionally, until they are browned on all sides, about 5 to 7 minutes (they may not be fully cooked yet, but that's okay). Transfer them to a plate and set aside while you make the sauce.

To make the sauce: Add the onion, green pepper, and garlic to the pan and sauté for about 5 minutes, or until softened. Deglaze the pan by adding the sherry and stirring to lift any browned bits off of the bottom of the pan. Add the crushed tomatoes, smoked paprika, and salt and pepper to taste. Add the meatballs back into the sauce, cover the pan, and reduce the heat to low. Let simmer for 15 minutes to finish cooking the meatballs and let the flavors meld together.

Yield: 6 servings

CHEF'S TIP

Can't find ground lamb? Ground turkey, pork, beef, or veal would all be delicious substitutes.

ALMOND SAFFRON CHICKEN

•Soy-free •Dairy-free

**This unique dish features a rich creamy sauce thickened with a hard-boiled egg.
Saffron lends a delicate complexity that I just love.**

1 pound (454 g) boneless, skinless chicken thighs, cut into 1-inch (2.5 cm) cubes

Salt and pepper to taste

2 teaspoons olive oil, divided

5 cloves garlic

½ cup (74 g) whole almonds

1 hard-boiled egg, peeled

½ cup (120 ml) dry sherry

1½ cups (355 ml) chicken stock

1 pinch saffron threads

Heat a large, heavy-bottomed sauté pan over high heat. Season the chicken generously with salt and pepper. Place 1 teaspoon of the olive oil in the pan, then add the chicken. Let cook for 5 minutes, then turn the chicken and let cook for 5 more minutes, until evenly browned. Transfer the chicken to a plate and set aside.

Lower the heat to medium. Add the remaining 1 teaspoon olive oil, whole garlic cloves, and almonds to the pan. Cook, stirring occasionally, until the almonds and garlic begin to get golden brown spots on them and become fragrant.

Place the almonds and garlic, hard-boiled egg, sherry, chicken stock, and saffron into a blender. Blend on high until the mixture is smooth and creamy. Return the chicken to the sauté pan and pour the almond sauce over the chicken. Cook over low heat, stirring occasionally, for 15 to 20 minutes, or until the chicken is tender and the sauce has thickened slightly.

Yield: 6 servings

CHEF'S TIP

Saffron is tasty, but it can be expensive. If you want to skip it, try a small pinch of turmeric to add a golden hue.

RED SANGRIA

•Soy-free •Dairy-free •Nut-free

Choose a fairly inexpensive dry red wine for this recipe. This recipe is for one pitcher, but for a party of six, I usually make at least three pitchers!

¼ cup (50 g) sugar

¼ cup (60 ml) hot water

1 bottle (750 ml) red wine, such as Rioja or cabernet

¼ cup (60 ml) brandy

¼ cup (60 ml) Triple Sec

½ cup (120 ml) orange juice

1 green apple, cored and cut into ½-inch (1.3 cm) cubes

1 orange, sliced into rounds, then quartered

Ice as needed

Place the sugar in a pitcher and add the hot water. Stir until dissolved. Add the wine, brandy, Triple Sec, orange juice, apple, and orange.

Let sit for at least 1 hour to allow the flavors to blend. Before serving, top the pitcher off with ice and serve with a wooden spoon in the pitcher to help portion some of the fruit into each glass while pouring.

Yield: 6 servings

CHEF'S TIP

In the summertime, I replace the apple and orange with about 1½ cups (215 g) blackberries, raspberries, or sliced strawberries for a fresh, seasonal variation.

CREAMY COCONUT FLAN

•Soy-free •Nut-free

Flan is a baked custard with a creamy consistency and a golden caramel sauce that is rich and sweet. Garnish this with toasted coconut to make it extra special.

½ cup (100 g) granulated sugar

4 eggs

1 cup (235 ml) half-and-half

1 can (14 ounces, or 400 ml) coconut milk

1 can (14 ounces, or 400 ml) sweetened condensed milk

1 tablespoon (15 ml) vanilla extract

Preheat the oven to 325°F (170°C, or gas mark 3).

Place the sugar in a small saucepan over medium-high heat. Cook without stirring for about 5 to 6 minutes, or until melted and caramelized to a golden brown color. Pour into the bottom of a deep-dish pie plate, quickly swirling to coat the bottom of the pan with the sugar.

Combine the eggs, half-and-half, coconut milk, sweetened condensed milk, and vanilla in a blender. Blend until smooth and creamy and pour into the pie plate.

Fill a large pan with 1 inch (2.5 cm) of very hot water. Place the pie plate inside the water bath and place into the oven. The water bath will help the flan cook evenly.

Bake for 1 hour to 1 hour and 15 minutes, or until the flan is set and only jiggles slightly.

Remove from the oven and the water bath. Let cool to room temperature. Refrigerate for several hours until cold. To unmold the flan, run a sharp knife around the perimeter of the flan to loosen it from the pie plate. Place a large flat serving plate on top of the pie plate, then quickly and carefully invert the pie plate so that the flan is now on the plate. Carefully lift the pie plate off of the flan. The caramel has formed a sauce that should flow over the flan.

Yield: 10 servings

CHEF'S TIP

Half-and-half is simply equal parts whole milk and cream. In this recipe, 1 cup (235 ml) half-and-half is equal to ½ cup (120 ml) milk and ½ cup (120 ml) cream.

Ladies' Lunch

SERVES 6

A social gathering on the patio or serious business both require delicious sustenance. Whatever the reason your ladies are getting together, they will appreciate the light and tasty recipes you serve from this menu.

....

THE MENU

Countdown to the Party Timeline

2 DAYS BEFORE THE PARTY:

○ Make a list and do the grocery shopping.

1 DAY BEFORE THE PARTY:

○ Make the Lemon Curd for the Berries with Lemon Curd.

○ Make the Caper Dressing for the Butter Lettuce Salad.

○ Make Sweet Tea for the Mint Juleps.

○ Set the table and decorate as desired.

THE DAY OF THE PARTY:

○ Make the Cucumber Sandwiches with Goat Cheese, Watercress, and Radish.

○ Make the Avocado Mousse for the Baked Crab Cakes.

○ Make the crab cakes but do not bake them yet. Refrigerate until needed.

○ Take out and arrange all the liquors and ingredients for the Sweet Tea Mint Juleps.

1 HOUR BEFORE:

○ Bake the crab cakes.

○ Prepare the Butter Lettuce Salad.

○ Prepare the berries to serve with the Lemon Curd.

CUCUMBER SANDWICHES
WITH GOAT CHEESE, WATERCRESS, AND RADISH

•Soy-free •Nut-free

**Cucumber sandwiches are a classic for a ladies' lunch or tea. My version
is bread-free, but just as tasty!**

1 log (4 ounces, or 112 g) goat
cheese

1 large cucumber, peeled and sliced
into ¼-inch (6 mm) slices (you will
need 24 slices)

Salt and pepper to taste

½ cup (25 g) watercress, roughly
chopped

3 red radishes, thinly sliced

Cut the goat cheese into 12 even slices. Place 1 slice of goat cheese onto
12 cucumber slices. Sprinkle each one with salt and pepper. Top each with
a bit of watercress and a few slices of radish. Top each with the remaining
12 cucumber slices. Place on a platter and serve.

Yield: 12 sandwiches

CHEF'S TIP

Goat cheese is very soft, so to slice the goat cheese log into 12 pieces,
make sure it is very cold and use a 10-inch (25 cm) piece of unflavored
dental floss pulled taut between your fingers to slice the cheese.

BAKED CRAB CAKES

•Soy-free •Dairy-free •Nut-free

A coating of finely crushed corn flakes crisps beautifully in the oven,
so these baked crab cakes are just as good as any fried version. Instead of tartar sauce,
I serve these with the Avocado Mousse on page 23.

1 teaspoon olive oil

2 cloves garlic, minced

½ cup (80 g) diced onion

½ cup (60 g) diced celery

½ cup (75 g) diced red bell pepper

¼ cup (25 g) finely chopped scallion
(green parts only)

1 tablespoon (11 g) Dijon mustard

¼ cup (56 g) mayonnaise

4 teaspoons Old Bay seasoning

¼ teaspoon salt

2 teaspoons lemon zest

2 eggs

3 cups (102 g) corn flakes, finely
crushed, divided

1 pound (454 g) crabmeat, picked
over for shell fragments

Preheat the oven to 375°F (190°C, or gas mark 5). Grease a baking sheet
and set aside.

Heat a medium-size sauté pan over medium-high heat. Add the olive
oil, garlic, onion, celery, and red bell pepper and cook for 5 to 7 minutes,
until softened. Place the softened vegetables in a large mixing bowl.

Add the chopped scallion, Dijon, mayonnaise, Old Bay seasoning,
salt, lemon zest, eggs, and 1 cup (34 g) of the crushed corn flakes to the
bowl. Stir to combine. Add the crabmeat and stir gently to combine the
ingredients but not break up any of the lumps of crab.

Form the mixture into 6 patties. Place the remaining 2 cups (68 g) corn
flakes on a plate. Gently coat each crab cake in the corn flakes and place
onto the greased baking sheet. Spray the crab cakes lightly with nonstick
spray and bake for 20 to 25 minutes, or until golden on the outside and
heated through.

Yield: 6 servings

CHEF'S TIPS

• Jumbo lump crabmeat is ideal to use because the pieces of crab are large
  and succulent. Lump crabmeat or claw crabmeat are really good, too, and
  make a more affordable alternative if jumbo lump isn't in your budget.

• Make sure the corn flakes you use are gluten-free. Sometimes they have
  added gluten-containing ingredients.

FRESH BERRIES
WITH LEMON CURD

•Soy-free •Nut-free

**Delicious, fresh, and simple, these desserts are great not just
with a ladies' lunch, but at any time.**

¾ cup (180 ml) lemon juice

1 tablespoon (6 g) lemon zest

6 egg yolks

1 cup (200 g) sugar

2 teaspoons cornstarch

6 tablespoons (84 g) cold
unsalted butter

1 cup (145 g) strawberries,
quartered

1 cup (145 g) blueberries

1 cup (125 g) raspberries

Combine the lemon juice, lemon zest, egg yolks, sugar, and cornstarch
in a medium-size saucepan. Turn the heat on to medium, and whisk the
ingredients until the mixture begins to slowly thicken.

Keep whisking, watching the mixture carefully to avoid overheating
the mixture and curdling the eggs. This should take about 10 minutes to
thicken. You will know it is thick enough when the mixture coats the back
of a spoon, and the mixture doesn't run when you drag your finger down
the back of the spoon.

Remove from the heat, and add the butter, 1 tablespoon (14 g) at a time,
until fully incorporated and melted. Chill the mixture for several hours until
very cold (the mixture will thicken even further).

Serve a dollop of lemon curd in a dessert glass and top with the berries.

Yield: 6 servings

CHEF'S TIP
Use limes instead of lemons for a tangy lime curd!

BUTTER LETTUCE SALAD
WITH CAPER DRESSING

•Soy-free •Dairy-free •Nut-free

I love salads of simple greens tossed with a delicious dressing. Feel free to dress this salad up with additional veggies, if you like.

1 clove garlic, finely minced

1 tablespoon (11 g) Dijon mustard

2 tablespoons (30 ml) red or white wine vinegar

¼ cup (60 ml) olive oil

1 tablespoon (8 g) capers, roughly chopped

Salt and pepper to taste

2 heads butter lettuce, washed, dried, and torn into bite-size pieces

In a small bowl, whisk together the garlic, Dijon, and vinegar. Add the olive oil and whisk until incorporated. Stir in the capers, and season to taste with salt and pepper. Toss the desired amount of dressing with the lettuce and serve.

Yield: 6 servings

CHEF'S TIP

Capers are salty, so be mindful of the amount of salt you add to the dressing—you may need less than you think.

SWEET TEA MINT JULEP

•Soy-free •Dairy-free •Nut-free

Two Southern classics combine here into one perfect cocktail. True sweet-tea connoisseurs debate which kind of tea to use. I think Lipton or Luzianne both work great.

FOR SWEET TEA:
4 black tea bags

2½ cups (588 ml) boiling water

⅓ cup (66 g) sugar

FOR MINT JULEP:
1 cup (235 g) crushed ice

4 mint sprigs

1 ounce (28 ml) bourbon

To make the sweet tea: Combine the tea bags with the boiling water. Let steep for 10 minutes. Add the sugar and stir to dissolve. Remove the tea bags and chill.

To make the mint julep: Put the crushed ice into a cocktail shaker along with the mint, bourbon, and ¼ cup (60 ml) of the sweet tea. Shake to chill and bring out the flavor of the mint. Pour the drink along with the crushed ice into a tall glass and serve with a straw.

Yield: 1 serving

CHEF'S TIP

Feel free to double the recipe for the sweet tea to offer to guests who choose not to have a cocktail.

ACKNOWLEDGMENTS

Many thanks to the team at Fair Winds for another book I can be proud of. Thank you to my agent, Marilyn Allen, for your continued guidance. Gratitude to Theresa Raffetto for working so hard to do the photos for this book on my turf; your work is beautiful. Thanks to Jessica Gorman and Deborah Williams for your gorgeous styling. Thanks to Dara Lyubinsky and Regina Hilton for your expertise. Thanks to David Youdovin and Jessica Levine for your support and open arms.

Jen Siemon, what would I do without you? Thank you, thank you, thank you for your talent, your time, and your incredible friendship. Thanks to Whitney Houser for your support while I wrote this book, and for taking such big bites that let me know when I finally got a recipe right. To Gerard Dupin, Chris Gushard, Wayne Gushard, Virginia Hinrichsen, Rachel Weaver, Peter Dupin, and the rest of my family, thank you for the love and support that keeps me going!

ABOUT THE AUTHOR

Olivia Dupin is a private chef, recipe developer, and consultant. Since being diagnosed with celiac disease in 2009, she has been committed to creating simple, delicious, gluten-free recipes so that those with restrictions can still enjoy the foods they love.

Olivia is a graduate of the Culinary Institute of America and has worked as a private chef to clients such as professional baseball player Mark Teixeira of the New York Yankees and comedian and television star Jerry Seinfeld.

Olivia maintains a recipe blog dedicated to simple, home-style, gluten-free recipes at www.livglutenfree.com. She lives, cooks, and writes in Jersey City, New Jersey.

INDEX BY RECIPE TYPE

INDEX